Combing Cotton

Also by Robin Wilson

Clean Design: Wellness for Your Lifestyle
(Greenleaf, 2015)

Kennedy Green House: From the Foundation to the Furnishings
(Greenleaf, 2010)

Combing Cotton

Transform Your Ancestry Into Your Competitive Advantage

Robin Wilson

MATT HOLT

Matt Holt Books
An Imprint of BenBella Books, Inc.
Dallas, TX

The events, locations, and conversations in this book, while true, are re-created from the author's memory. However, the essence of the story, and the feelings and emotions evoked, are intended to be accurate representations. In certain instances, names, persons, organizations, and places have been changed to protect an individual's privacy.

MATT HOLT BENBELLA

Matt Holt is an imprint of BenBella Books, Inc.
BenBella Books, Inc.
8080 N. Central Expressway
Suite 1700
Dallas, TX 75206
benbellabooks.com
Send feedback to feedback@benbellabooks.com

Printed in the United States of America
10 9 8 7 6 5 4 3 2 1

Library of Congress Control Number: 2026018737
ISBN 9781637749821 (hardcover)
ISBN 9781637749838 (electronic)

Editing by Lydia Choi
Copyediting by Shelby Harbour
Proofreading by Sarah Vostok and Jenny Bridges
Text design and composition by Jordan Koluch
Weave icon by Candy Design from Noun Project (CC BY 3.0)
Cover design by Jason Arias, image © Adobe Stock / Robert
Printed by Lake Book Manufacturing

Fifteen years ago, I published my first book on design as a single woman living in New York City on the thirty-third floor of an apartment overlooking the East River. And then my second book on the topic of wellness was published in the midst of a divorce, while living in suburban New Jersey with my toddler.

This book was finished with my newly minted teenage daughter, who amazes me each day with her intellect, humor, beauty, kindness, and athleticism—she has taught me that motherhood requires resilience and gratitude for every milestone along the journey.

This book is dedicated to my daughter, my parents, and the friends and family who have been part of this life journey—especially my child's godparents, Cheryl and Joy, who have become "sister-friends" over the decades. And thank you to those who ran toward me and my daughter—with advice, food, funds, and friendship, instead of sitting idly on the gossip sidelines. *I remember only being able to afford a cupcake for her second birthday after we fled . . .*

As of the writing of this book, my company has built a global brand of textiles, products for home and body, and items sold at both retail and wholesale through licensing and partnerships.

With immense gratitude, I salute the ancestors who paved the way for me to achieve my wildest dreams in ways that might once have been thought to be impossible—my achievements reflect dreams that my ancestors hoped for, even though they would never meet their great-great-grandchildren or great-great-niece! Their faith in the future resonates in my success.

And finally: I made a Bucket List at nineteen, and it is the report card of my life of "wishes" that continue to come true . . . so grateful for these life experiences!

—Robin

Contents

ACKNOWLEDGMENTS

I am grateful to so many people and wanted to call out a few:

Thank you, Dr. Joy Touchstone, a leading pediatrician in Texas, for being a great childhood friend since second grade and my daughter's godmother. I am so grateful that your brother and my brother grew up as school friends.

Thank you, Dr. Cheryl Dorsey, of Echoing Green, for being my sister-friend and my daughter's godmother. You were there in the first days after her birth and have been a dear friend since I was twenty years old and moved to Boston!

Thank you to Boston friends: Bennie Wiley, Nina Doggett, Pam Everhart, Sandra Sims-Williams, Irma Tyler-Wood, Kim Budd, Marti Wilson-Taylor, Eric Collins, James Down, Rikk Larsen, Dr. Augustus White, Ray Shepard, Kim (Smedvig) Taylor, Tom Waye, and so many others in Boston who made my early twenties special with kindness, guidance, patience, and wisdom.

Thank you to our ancestor Maya Angelou for having me at one of your Thanksgiving celebrations in North Carolina, and for when you and Cicely Tyson told me, "He [my date] wasn't the one" (you were right!). And then you told me to "remember that my calling is not a job, but what I was put here to do . . . and to always take a seat at the table." I cherish that memory of your voice calling me over to sit with you . . .

ACKNOWLEDGMENTS

Thank you to Renee Warren, my first friend in New York, who made sure that the city felt like a village. Thank you for being the first visitor to the hospital after my daughter's birth.

Thank you to Adam Glassman from *O* Magazine for calling me in 2004 and guiding me to "put my name in my business and to believe in myself." You changed my life when you gave me visibility in the magazine and book. In 2020, when we rebranded, we did it so that we could go to the next level, and for fifteen years, we have honored your prescient advice.

Thank you to those who know how much you did for me after the divorce: Eleonor, Mimi, Mayida, Stacy, Patricia, Denise, Barbara, Maria, Robert, Peter, and Ryan. I remain so grateful!

Thank you to the people who protected the business: Peter Harvey, Esq., Chaim Book, Esq., Steven Delsanto, CPA, Jennifer Hickman, and all the friends and family investors.

And thank you to my Austin influences: relatives, pediatrician, schoolteachers, Jerry Lawson, Connie Lucas, Susi Ferguson, Stephanie Roberts, Camille (Shannon) Hudson, Jacquetta (Nammar) Feldman, the Ruiz family, and the Treadwell, Washington, and Cannatti families.

There are so many other folks that it would take pages . . . so THANK YOU!

Preface: Origin Story

Did you know that one bale of cotton can make:

- 215 pairs of jeans
- 249 bedsheets
- 690 bath towels
- 1,217 T-shirts
- 313,600 $100 bills*

In this book, you will meet Polly, age four—human cargo on the brigantine ship the *Planter*—who arrived in the Port of New Orleans in 1819. She was my maternal fourth great-grandmother, and the manifest said that the "cargo" origin was Africa.

And you meet me, her fourth great-granddaughter—someone who created a global brand with both durable and soft goods sold at retail, wholesale, and to the US

---

* "What Can You Make from a Bale of Cotton?" National Cotton Council of America, accessed March 16, 2026, https://www.cotton.org/pubs/cottoncounts/what-can-you-make.cfm.

military—generating over $100 million (wholesale) in licensed brand revenue since 2000.

Think of cotton as a metaphor for our lives. The process of combing cotton stretches a plant to reach its highest potential. The very process is a metaphor reflecting how we must often stretch ourselves so we can become our best selves. In the process, we honor our ancestors—those who dreamed and worked so hard for future great-grandchildren they might not ever meet.

Combing Cotton shares a life story about the piecework quilt of my life with a central theme of resilience—choices, challenges, regrets, successes, failures, and the serendipitous moments that made my very existence possible: the meet-cute of my parents, the resourcefulness of my grandparents, the Middle Passage taken by Polly and the Pilgrims.

The warp and weft of my family history is emblematic of American history, containing the central tenets of work ethic, entrepreneurship, education, morals, values, creativity . . . a perfectly imperfect family!

We are all born perfect—soft and pure—just as a cotton boll looks perfect from a distance. But life begins to happen, and the exterior can get prickly. Ingredients are added—sometimes detritus—like the bugs and leaves and insects in the cotton boll. And just like with cotton, as we mature, we must comb ourselves to get stuff out, sometimes with therapy and introspection, sometimes with moving away for a fresh start.

We only reach our highest potential when we examine our lives, focusing on resilience—similar to the process of stretching, ginning, and processing cotton into fabric. Repeating this combing process makes us stronger, more resilient, and just like fabric, we can show the world our highest potential.

But only after we comb the cotton to strengthen our

awareness of self—or take the time to comb the "bugs" out of our life—will we reach or exceed the heights that our ancestors dreamt for us.

Think about a grandparent or elder in your community who paved the way by showing a belief in you. Through their words or actions, they planted a seed for your future so you could achieve your dreams! They may not have lived to see it come true, but they had faith you could achieve *if you wanted to.* Sometimes they did not know how you would accomplish it, but they encouraged you to believe that you would, could, and should try.

So now, get ready to turn the pages and learn how the process of combing cotton can be a metaphor to change your life . . .

Part 1

Raw Material

Chapter 1

SEEDS

Cotton seeds are planted in spring after the last frost and require a warm climate, ample sunlight, and a long growing season. Dormancy is the natural state of suspended growth in a mature seed, lasting from a few months to many years. This state allows a seed to survive through unfavorable conditions while waiting for the optimal environment for growth. Planting seeds in the right conditions will allow them to emerge.

My dad told the story of watching a college girl tuck her books under her arms like a football to sprint after the city bus with a swinging purse while wearing pumps and a pencil skirt. She regularly ran late when rushing from campus to her off-campus work study job. My dad said that he thought she was cute, but he was shy. And he did not think a college girl would have any interest in a city bus driver with just a high school education, who still lived at home with his parents. But he decided to try to catch her eye—and started making his sandwich break at her college stop.

Soon, the girl would be about to tuck her books for a sprint to catch the bus, but the bus was always there on the days he worked. With a breathless "thank you," she would sit in the front seat. And over time, those thank-yous evolved into conversation, and finally, he asked her out on a date. So, with the whoosh of a bus door—and with the help of a sandwich break—my mom stepped into his life!

Dad had been fortunate to be one of the first three Black bus drivers hired by the city of Austin in the late 1960s, which was the beginning of his dream for a solid middle-class lifestyle. In 1967, my dad was assigned the East Austin Campus route.

In 1966, my mom enrolled at Huston-Tillotson College, an HBCU located in Austin. Her older sisters had graduated from Houston-area universities. Because one of her brothers and his wife lived in Austin, my mom moved into an extra room at their home.

In 1969, they eloped, just the two of them—Rubin and Jo Ann. And a few months later, in September, I was born. When they wed, she was twenty-two and he was twenty-nine.

I categorize my father's family as the warp (strength) and my mother's family as the weft (style). And knitting has pulled together an ancestral quilt which informs my life journey so that I can honor my ancestors with a strong work ethic, building on their legacy, and reaching back to help others realize their dreams.

MATERNAL SIDE

My mom was born in Angleton, Texas, in 1947 as a middle child in a family of six children. She was from a respected, country rich family that owned several businesses and significant real estate. Her father maintained the real estate holdings of my great-grandfather, a fair-skinned man who often "passed" when he went into Houston to conduct business with his blue eyes and a smattering of freckles. His attorney father was of Irish descent and had a separate family in Houston. And he would facilitate real estate deals and vouch for his son so that he could buy property, including much of the land near Rice University, allowing him to build wealth with a portfolio of parking lots and rental properties.

My great-grandfather was an entrepreneur, my grandfather was an entrepreneur, but his children did not maintain the generational wealth—it is often called the "curse of the third" because they often have different ambitions due to a less hardscrabble upbringing. I am part of the fourth generation, which often has a few who reinvigorate the entrepreneurial mindset.

My mother's side of the family can trace their ancestry back to the fifteenth century in Europe. And when we traced our family history, we learned that some members of her family were part of the British royal family, while others were participants in the Boston Tea Party rebellion, and Benjamin Franklin shows up in the family tree as a distant cousin.

Through DNA, we actually can see the time frame when certain members of her family lineage "became brown" in Mississippi in the 1800s. Many in my mother's family were Freedmen, and some gained this status in the early 1800s with their military service in the Texas-Mexico War, and some ended the 1870s as Buffalo Soldiers after the Civil War. With their military service, many ascended to become part of the merchant class as landowners, entrepreneurs, and educators in the Houston area.

The first documented enslaved person from Africa was named Polly—my maternal fourth great-grandmother. According to the slave manifest, the *Planter* ship arrived in 1819 to the Port of New Orleans. Polly was only four years old—documented as cargo, not as a passenger. Polly was likely not her real name. No last name. No true date of birth, only an estimate of the year 1815, given on a slave manifest. No birthplace or birth country. Just a continent. A listing showing Africa as the origin and New Orleans as the destination port.

Can you imagine a toddler spending months on a Middle Passage voyage? Imagine how her sea legs had to adjust to the land. A toddler, trying to regain her land legs. Clothing in tatters. Likely rags—made of cotton.

Whoever wrote the flourishing feather-quill writing on the manifest records only cared about the "cargo," not the human toll of a toddler with no guardian. Did the person writing the cargo details care or notice that there was no mention of a parent? Who had she been ripped away from? Did her parents die on the five-thousand-mile journey? Did she have any memories of her parents or grandparents? What were her first memories? Had she any memory of sleeping in a bed? Or a memory of eating a fresh vegetable? How much fear enveloped her? Was she separated from her family at the dock? Was she crying as the slave auctioneer pointed her away from those who cared for her? We will never know because few people wanted to discuss this painful time with their grandchildren, so the oral history has been lost.

Remember that in 1807, Congress abolished the foreign slave trade—a ban that went into effect on January 1, 1808. After this date, importing enslaved people from Africa became illegal in the United States. It should be noted that eleven years later, Polly arrived in New Orleans in 1819!

We will never know how Polly was traded or sold to someone and ended up in Texas. But we do know that she was among the last humans to find out when slavery in the United States was abolished, as the news didn't reach Texas until June 19, 1865, when freedom was proclaimed in Galveston. Hence, my family has celebrated Juneteenth for generations—long before it was named a federally recognized national holiday in 2021.

Elders who grew up in Jim Crow Texas knew that the only path forward, in some cases, was to be respected in the community. It was a way to prevent an undesirable outcome from something as simple as being pulled over at a traffic stop.

Great Granddaddy made his money in real estate, and his son (my grandfather!), continued the generational wealth by preserving and increasing holdings. Remember that Great Granddaddy was light-skinned with blue eyes, and his son, my grandfather, had a darker skin tone. So, on behalf of Mr. Scott (his dad!), he would make the rounds in an old, beat-up pickup truck—with his nice truck parked in the country. He would wear coveralls to collect rent from tenants and get proceeds from the parking lot change boxes on land owned by the family. Or he would drive his father as a "chauffeur" since Great Granddaddy never learned to drive.

The white parking lot managers did not know that my grandfather was actually the son of the owner. And my grandfather played the role of a trusted errand person with a lot of "yes sirs" and a smile. These managers were typically polite because the "owner" trusted this man. Family lore said that everyone called him "man" because he refused to be called "boy" during the Jim Crow era.

Great Granddaddy had eighteen children due to the deaths in childbirth of his first two wives and marrying a woman who already had children (who he raised as his own!). He made sure that everyone understood that being an entrepreneur was a way for economic freedom, and many of his children pursued business ownership. His son (my grandfather) maintained the businesses and also expanded holdings to include commercial real estate, a general store and laundromat, and a janitorial company that cleaned the small town's bank, courthouse, and police station, plus one venture providing landscaping services and ranch hands serving the business leaders—the very individuals who could impact your family destiny and afforded a certain level of privilege when you are known to be from a "good family" in a country town.

Great Granddaddy always said, "Your word is your bond. Your family name means everything. You can do bad business with good people, but you can never do good business with bad people."

I called my maternal grandmother Granny, and she shopped at the best stores: Sakowitz, Palais Royal, and Neiman Marcus. She wore hats, gloves, and a Cartier watch. She vacationed and did missionary work while visiting Israel, Europe, Russia, and the Caribbean. With her light skin and blue-gray eyes, she moved unimpeded through her days with the understanding that she could pass if needed. She simply never articulated her race—always saying that she was "part of the human race" when traveling globally. She also said that telling people she was a Texan often opened more doors because of global curiosity about the state!

Granny's life did not start out that way. She told a story with tears in her eyes about her last memory of her mother around age ten, when she disappeared one night. Her mother and her three daughters, including Granny, were living in East Texas in a rural cottage. They heard horses galloping in the woods and a commotion outside their home. Her mother shushed them and told them to hide under the bed. Her mother sternly told them, "And don't come out until I tell you to." And then she left the bedroom, closing the door behind her.

The girls heard muffled voices at the front door, a scuffle, and then silence. Granny and her sisters hid under the bed for a very long time. They never saw their mother again. The rumor around town was that the Klan got her, but she never learned the truth. She searched for her mother for the rest of her life with private detectives but never found a trace of her.

Granny was raised by other relatives, and it seems that she and her sisters moved around a lot, but she would rarely speak about any memories she wanted to share about her childhood. She and her sisters remained very close, and they all married entrepreneurial men. Her mindset was focused on the belief that religion, decorum, manners, and education made anything possible.

When she married my grandfather—an entrepreneur who

was very involved in the church—she understood her role as part of a family of some means that was respected in the community. With indomitable optimism, both she and my grandfather worked to achieve their goals together, and every day she made sure that he had a hot lunch and dinner—and the one question they always asked was "What's right?" instead of the other question: "What's wrong?" It taught all of the children to focus on the positive before the negative.

They had six children, all of whom graduated from high school and attended college. All of them worked during high school and summers to learn a segment of the business. And when they went to college, they were able to decide a major based on real-life work experience. And their higher education resulted in one lawyer, one MBA, one teacher, one engineer, one pharmacist, and my mom, who continued to manage a portion of the real estate and laundromat business while also working in law enforcement.

PATERNAL SIDE

In 1894, my paternal grandfather, whom I called Grandpapa, was born into a cotton sharecropping family. He was a World War I veteran with an eighth-grade education, and he could only get a job building the railroad across Texas and seasonal sharecropping. He did not benefit much from his military service, save access to the abysmal segregated VA Hospital in Temple, Texas, for medical treatments if he could get an appointment. Some of his siblings became successful in business, but his branch of the family remained largely poor.

The saddest story I heard was about their son, George, who

was two years older than my dad. George was scalded as a toddler in the tar-paper sharecropper shack. When a whites-only hospital about ten minutes away refused to treat the burns suffered, they ran to borrow a neighbor's Model T car and then drove thirty miles away to a colored hospital. Little George died on the way.

That loss scarred my grandparents and made them realize that it was time to do whatever it took to get out of Littig. My father was born in 1940 as the youngest of ten children and often spoke of the sadness in the eyes of his mother, who sometimes referenced "poor George" with tears in her eyes before hugging him tighter. He knew at an early age how much he was loved!

Dad experienced a different life from his older siblings because he only had to work for two harvests at age four and five—where he only had to pick one twenty-five-pound bag of cotton each day. Dad remembered being a shoeless child at age five, picking cotton and missing the first few weeks of school in Littig.

Grandpapa's adult sons (my dad's older brothers) entered the military beginning in WWII, sending money home to free the family from the tyranny of an oppressive cotton sharecropper system. The sacrifices of Dad's older brothers—my uncles—whose military service ended with the Korean War, made his life journey different from that of his siblings.

Each adult son sent funds home to buy out the shares from the landowner. It took five years, but this allowed the Wilson family an opportunity to buy a house on East 17th Street in Austin between 1946 and 1947, when Airport Boulevard was still a gravel road, according to my father. They had to pay in cash for their home because banks had redlined the area.

The legacy of the Austin, Texas, 1928 Master Plan officially forced Black residents to live in East Austin and banned access to certain public parks. Through zoning policies and discriminatory private deed restrictions, it was prohibited for non-white people to own or occupy land in the rest of the city.

It is ironic that my dad became an Austin city bus driver, as there were rules prior to November 2, 1961, that all people of color had to "move to the back of the bus at Congress Avenue," which was the downtown nexus at the State Capitol. My father remembers an instance of riding the city bus as a child, when he and his brother were younger than nine years old. They did not move fast enough for an older white man, who yelled that the N-word needed to move quicker to "go where you belong" as he whacked my uncle on the side of the head with a cane, leaving a lifetime scar.

Psychological wounds existed for my uncles who returned home from military service and rightfully expected to receive the GI Bill and good jobs to uplift their station in life. They would share stories about how they had sent a portion of their checks home to help the family buy a house—to uplift the family—risking their lives for the country with military service. But when they returned to Texas, each of them found that the GI Bill—originally the Servicemen's Readjustment Act of 1944—was systematically denied to Black veterans. In Texas, white segregationists ran the state, and local agencies tasked to administer the bill's benefits on behalf of the federal government used their position of power to deny or delay the benefits until they expired. Even if the agency administrators dealt with Black veterans fairly, the veterans ran into an additional barrier: housing discrimination.

Veterans were supposed to have access to low-interest mortgages through the US Department of Veterans Affairs (VA), but both bank policies and federal rules prohibited loans in areas that were redlined and considered to be "undesirable" neighborhoods. According to historical records, the VA would reject mortgage applications from Black veterans outright, even when they met all the qualifications. And real estate agents and developers kept Black families out of "desirable" areas to maintain segregation, so treatment was not equal or inclusive for veterans in that era.

One of my uncles received an associate's degree and was a decorated veteran. When he applied for a job at the post office, he was only offered a janitorial role, even though others with lesser education were given managerial offers. He bitterly blamed much of his lifetime hardship on the frustration of serving his country and not receiving any of the benefits promised, except access to subpar VA services requiring months of waiting for a checkup at the segregated Temple VA Hospital.

So after military service, most of my father's brothers headed west to California, where they sought to build lives that more closely matched their dreams and what they thought would be a less discriminatory community. But without a formal education, most of their lives as longshoremen simply meant more hard work and living in redlined neighborhoods in Oakland. These uncles would visit Texas for the regular Juneteenth reunion, and each of them would repeat to our generation, "Get your education," amid tales of their limited opportunities to advance.

In fact, one of my father's cousins, Susie Green, enrolled at the University of Texas in 1956 after the 1954 *Brown v. Board of Education* ruling, which allowed the first Black undergraduates to attend the school. She soon left campus due to racial animus and unequal conditions, moving to Los Angeles in the hope of a better life. Both she and my father's sister who went to college were strong voices in telling our generation to "get your education," no matter what!

My dad's mom, Pearline, whom I called Grandmother, began her life in the Belton, Texas, area to an unwed mother. Oral history tales and a DNA test confirm her mother was a Native American. It is clear that with an education and a different set of circumstances, my grandmother could have had a different life with her long, straight hair and light brown eyes. She was raised with her aunts who were close to her age, Hattie and Martha (my great-great-aunts), who were even more fair with blue eyes, and all of them had long, straight hair, even in the worst humidity. Her sisters traveled the world; looking back, I realize that there had to be instances where they "passed" to have such experiences.

My grandmother became a 1950s housekeeper who rode the city bus in a uniform to West Austin—moving to the back of the bus after it crossed Congress Avenue—to cook, clean, and care for white families. She wore her hair in a tight bun.

Her recipes were prized, and she was regularly poached by other families, leading to a full schedule with multiple households, which would often lead to a salary increase. She also created cleaning solutions that used household products: vinegar, lemon, toothpaste, Coca-Cola, and baking soda.

At the same time, she suffered the indignity of having to carry her own separate dish, utensils, and cup because the families did not want her to eat or drink from their dishware. It was so ironic, given that she made food the family ate and cleaned their dishes, made their beds, and ironed their garments—and cared for their babies.

She also dealt with sadness around some children she had comforted and cared for since birth—until they "became mean" after a certain age. Children who loved her so much as babies and toddlers, until they reached a certain age when they were taught that she was not to be loved. She understood being treated as the help, yet set a boundary to respect herself when children called her racial epithets they were taught—which would often be the last day she chose to work for that family. However, she worked with some families over decades, and those families treated her with kindness and respect, and even attended her funeral.

After long days, she would return home to care for her own family and home. Plus, she would often have a commission for a new dress, mending, or other textile work requiring late-night work at the sewing machine. My father always said that his mother had the ability to sew like a couturier, using a photo, not a pattern. She only received a pittance of the deserved compensation for extra services because she did not think of herself as an entrepreneur, so she did not know how to price her talented work.

Again, the message from her was always: "Get your education."

> The pessimist sees the difficulty in every opportunity.
> The optimist sees the opportunity in every difficulty.
>
> —Winston Churchill

An optimistic mindset kept my paternal grandparents focused on ending their sharecropper servitude. They knew that their three youngest children would have different opportunities with a good education. And homeownership propelled the family into the lower middle class—not as renters, but as owners. All of their adult children helped pay for the house, and they called it "the homestead" once the family moved to Austin.

My dad's opportunities in life changed instantly as a "city kid" with their new home and full-year education. He started second grade at a segregated public school, Rosewood Elementary, and then moved to Kealing Middle School, and eventually graduated from L.C. Anderson High School. Dad became the third in the family to graduate from high school on time.

He had a work ethic that was quite ambitious and held two part-time jobs while in high school: after school as a filling station attendant, and as a weekend salad maker at Hoffbrau Steakhouse. While in high school, he bought a broken-down Chevrolet and fixed the engine. He said that some guys made fun of his car due to the rust spots and missing hubcaps, but he laughed at them by reminding them that he was "on wheels, and they were on foot," and then he would gun the engine and peel rubber as he drove away. This type of interaction was a hallmark of his sense of humor—a joke based on facts that point out ironic circumstances.

After high school graduation he did not go to college, but instead had three jobs: His filling station job became an evening role, his day job was delivering mail for state offices on a three-wheel scooter, and he continued the weekend salad maker shift at Hoffbrau Steakhouse, where he would see lawmakers, celebrities, and University of Texas coaches, but never Black patrons. They were not allowed in the restaurant due to Jim Crow laws:

Black patrons could pay full price and pick up their food in the alleyway.

Dad also spoke about how movie theaters did not let you in the front door—you bought your ticket at the kiosk and then walked around the back into the rat-infested alley to go through the back door to climb up the fire escape stairs to sit in the hot balcony, where the heat had risen. So Black patrons were often left sweating with no access to refreshments or a bathroom—while the AC worked on the main floor for other patrons: *Separate but equal.*

Dad continued to live at home, saving money, and his love of wheels persisted as he purchased a used Indian motorcycle from an Austin police officer. He later regretted selling it when the brand was discontinued, as it would have been a valuable vintage collectible. Two of his brothers became auto mechanics at Western Auto, and both of them bought homes in Austin, with the bachelor brother moving his parents in and turning "the homestead" into rental property.

Opportunity was sown by my paternal grandparents' decision to buy out their sharecropper lien, to move to Austin and to ensure that the youngest children in the family made a strong pivot toward education while maintaining a work ethic. Grandpapa maintained his love of the land by growing vegetables in the backyard garden to stretch their limited budget. And my grandmother made sure that she passed along the "art of homemaking" to her grandchildren—teaching me how to fold a fitted sheet and how to mend a quilt before I was seven years old!

Grandmother always said, "You may not have a lot of money, but you can keep a clean home that is nicely set up. Class is not about cost; it is about curating what you have."

In the weaving of cotton fabric, we need to understand the connection between knitting and the power of warp and weft. You cannot have durable fabric without interlocking loops, or both threads working together in complementary directions.

- Knitting raw cotton yarn creates connection by creating interlocking loops.
- Warp is the long, vertical threads on the loom, creating the strength, structure, and length of the fabric.
- Weft is the crosswise threads on the loom, providing strength and structure and connecting the style and beauty of the weave.

Dormant seeds are the origin story. These seeds are ready to germinate, and sometimes, over several years, they are ready to be fertilized.

My origin story reflects seeds that were laid in Europe and Africa. Seeds laid by my ancestors created a foundation over several generations, with examples of a strong work ethic and entrepreneurship. Because of this foundation, I faced many opportunities in my life that prepared me to build and create a lifestyle brand.

Information that was passed to me by my elders, details that were just understood: marketing, branding, pricing, partnerships, and philanthropy—all based on an ancestral foundation of entrepreneurship, business knowledge, homemaking tips, and an unstoppable work ethic. And that is what should be recognized as true generational wealth!

QUESTIONS TO COMB THROUGH

1. Which side of your family is the warp? And which is the weft?
2. Who was the first adult you remember who respected your opinion and validated your ideas?
3. Does your family come from humble beginnings, and are you now able to honor their hard work and dreams by uplifting them—or are you ashamed of your roots? How can you redefine your generational wealth as knowledge from elders?

Chapter 2

SPROUTS

Cotton sprouts are the initial leaves that emerge from a germinated seed and provide energy as the plant begins to establish roots. These seed leaves feed the young plant until the first "true leaves" take over energy production. And eventually, floral buds, known as squares, lead to familiar cotton bolls.

My parents' union brought together elegant style (Mom), work ethic (Dad), and generational wealth (knowledge of land, home, and commerce) from both sides. But it also knitted a genetic collision for me. "Everything's bigger in Texas," the saying goes . . . including allergies!

But could my ancestor hold the key: Polly, who disembarked at the Port of New Orleans? Did my allergies start with her reaction to a new land? Or could the genetic propensity have begun with my ancestors who worked in fields and who may have had a sensitivity to pollen, or with those who worked with animals and had a sensitivity to dander?

Both my parents had allergies—hay fever, eczema, a touch of asthma—and while pregnant, my mother was told by her OB-GYN that allergies had a strong genetic component, indicating that allergies might collide in their baby. According to my mom, as he closed her chart to signal the end of an appointment, he said, "Anyway, we might want to watch out for early signs of allergic reactions. With both of your sensitivities, she could have a double-whammy, or it could cancel out. We don't know." That was an understatement!

How severe would my allergies be? They would learn within hours of my birth.

My mom, almost eighty years old at the time of this writing, agreed to speak about my early days and upbringing in her own words:

> Even when I was pregnant, my OB-GYN doctor warned us that due to certain allergies my husband and I had, our baby was likely to be sensitive to the same things we were. And I'm forever grateful, even to this day, that the pediatrician was committed to natural medicine. That path began right there in the hospital when she was born—putting our daughter on the path to growing up strong and resilient.
>
> Because I was anemic and had other health concerns, breastfeeding Robin was not possible. So we decided to rely on formula, but she was allergic to it. With the first sip, she

turned beet red, had trouble breathing, and threw up. The hospital's task was to get us both stabilized.

Imagine being only twenty-two years old, and suddenly it was everything all at once. Imagine your new adult life, your marriage, your role as a mother, your newborn baby who can't keep anything down and has eczema. The best I could do was lean on the partners around me: my husband, my doctor, and my mother, who became my lifeline and a constant companion in those earliest days. My husband worked as a new driver at Kerrville Bus Company, and he was assigned a high-paying charter for a sports team, so he was on the road. I needed all the help that I could get because she was so sickly, and my anemia made me weak too. My mother came and made sure I ate and rested so that the baby could be nurtured.

I stayed in one room in the house. That was my domain, the small space I was responsible for. And my baby kept having one allergic reaction after another. Finally, we found through the process of elimination a soy-based formula that she could tolerate. We took careful notes for the pediatrician about what she ate and her reaction. The doctor finally settled on a mixture of goat's milk and formula.

In the first forty days, my job was to take care of the baby, and my mother took care of everything else. She was cleaning all the time. At first, family members and friends—who naturally wanted to come and see the baby—were told they could gradually come over. But my rules were different from those of most 1970s parents. I said no smoking, and to leave shoes outside. People thought I was crazy. My brother was a horse trainer, so he had barn smells all over him. He had to shower and change his clothes before he could hold the baby. She was so sensitive that if someone had a dog or a cat in their home, we would know it right away, as she would start to rub her eyes or wheeze. Overprotective: maybe. Caring: absolutely. Apologetic: never.

We were in a mad race to identify and remove triggers that would spike her temperature. We couldn't afford to race to the hospital with every reaction. So I gave her cooling baths and steamed up the bathroom so she could breathe. We were constantly trying to figure out what triggered a reaction so we could eliminate it from the environment or diet.

We developed a wonderful partnership with the hospital team: the doctor, the nurses, and the admissions office. The emergency room team knew us by name on sight. Everyone was cooperating to get us through this initial stage.

Her pediatrician was always merry and positive, and Robin loved his colorful neckties with cartoon characters. Early on, he gave us a choice that we never forgot: *"You can raise a strong child, or you can raise your child on strong medicine."*

We made that choice long ago, and it governed all our decisions regarding Robin's well-being throughout her entire childhood. There were so many times that we were awakened in the middle of the night and she could not breathe. It was terrifying for us as parents.

"Call my mom" were words that meant something when I was a child. It was my best, most reliable shield of defense. She would be there so quickly from her job when I was sitting in the school nurse's office and trying to catch my breath. There were allergic triggers that could take my breath away or cause a skin reaction, anything from carpet, animal dander, smoke, and dust to fragrances, food, soaps, lotions, detergents, and pollen. My mother was the main formidable force that stood between me and the rest of the world. Jokingly, it felt like I should be a bubble-wrapped child.

It was the 1970s and people smoked everywhere. She ignored the naysayers and created house rules: Smoking outside. Shoes off at the foyer. Homes with pets were off limits.

People with allergies and asthma are affected by one of the leading causes of death, with an average of 10 people dying daily in the United States.* Wiping down a surface does not eliminate the allergic trigger in the air, the saliva proteins, or the food residue, animal dander, or fur/hair on someone's clothing.

One of my most vivid childhood memories is the pediatrician's office. Dr. Williams wore funny neckties, and we went several times a week. He changed my life with what he called a newfangled approach: *microdosing*. His approach was to find a way to have me live a normal life over time by actually triggering a reaction in the safety of his office. He did skin tests, and then

* "Asthma Capitals: Health Outcomes That Impact Ranking," Asthma and Allergy Foundation of America, accessed March 19, 2026, https://aafa.org/asthma-allergy-research/our-research/asthma-capitals/asthma-health-outcomes/.

everything that I tested positive for, he exposed me to—from a pin-size amount to a spoonful.

Instead of the complete reduction of triggers, he believed that we should know the list of things that caused a reaction. He gradually introduced new triggers in his office to build a tolerance. If there was a reaction, he could immediately note and treat the symptoms. My mother and he consulted her notes, and by the time I was four, I knew every corner of his office. Over the years, he introduced foods and other items to recalibrate my immune system. There were many hours of waiting and powering through wheezing, hives, congestion, and fevers. But the reward came as I got older and met other children who had been on steroid medications and lived with very restrictive diets. My diet was actually increasing with small amounts of items previously off limits. I remember the first time I ate a half slice of pizza without a reaction was in my early teens.

Anything to *raise a strong child, and not a child on strong medicine* was the mantra. My mother and father had a limited budget, so they found ways to help me stay healthy and to keep breathing, including volunteering at the Wheatsville Co-op to get discounts on organic fruits and vegetables.

Medically, I had a care team that took their jobs seriously but maintained a happy space for a kid to feel optimism and positive thoughts. At some point, I was visiting Texas Children's Hospital in Houston and wandered into a pediatric cancer ward. My perspective became clear: I was only there for a few hours for some tests, and these other children were going through monthslong treatments. With that perspective and a positive focus, it became clear that my allergies may have felt like a burden, but it was a condition to simply manage and overcome, unlike other children who were suffering with invasive tests and a challenging prognosis.

Most people do not know that having allergies was not the only challenge I faced as a child. My mom remembers this time:

> Robin's allergic challenge was but one problem as a baby. The other issue we had to deal with was the fact that since I was quite petite and my husband was 6'4", she was unable to ever stretch out in utero. So she was born with bowlegs and a birth defect—a club foot—a foot so severely twisted at the ankle it was practically pointed the other way.
>
> Her pediatrician said other doctors might break a child's legs and place them in casts to correct them. And while it may work on the surface, some people could have other issues over time. His holistic approach involved deep tissue massage, braces, and orthopedic shoes—thus, training the bones and muscles. It took a lot of effort, but his approach was all about building my child up, not breaking her bones.
>
> He created a routine that had to be done in a certain order as she was growing, and that included stabilizing her musculoskeletal structure. She had to wear metal braces twenty-three hours a day, even to bed, with a rod between the shoes to hold her feet and legs in place. It was very painful to see, and we had to carry her everywhere initially so that she would get used to the braces before she learned to walk.
>
> Robin was a very smart baby, so true to her personality, she started doing things very early. As soon as she began to try to stand up, the pediatrician required a half-hour massage twice daily on her feet to get tendon muscles to relax. Then

> there were adjustments to the metal braces as they began to cut into her legs. The only time she was free from the braces was during a bath or the massages that I was taught to perform. She had to sleep flat on her back. When the rod was attached, she had to call out so that she could go to the bathroom at night.
>
> This was, of course, so difficult for all of us, especially my little baby girl. Watching the slow progress was actually painful, but she was so brave. It was all she knew, until she went to school . . . and that was when things got really challenging.

Each process was long and painful, but the doctor's approach allowed my body to work on itself—to reprogram itself to not think it was being invaded by certain foods or environmental triggers and to change the skeleton (my foundation) into a better structure. I call it the "working the bugs out" phase.

Bullying in the 1970s was mostly ignored by adults unless someone got hurt. Many adults called it teasing. The students called it poking fun. Some teachers turned their heads and let the kids work it out. But not my mom. She addressed it head-on with me.

She said from an early age that I was different, and I had to always remember that I must stand my ground, hold my head up, and never let words hurt me. Racial epithets and nasty comments were to be viewed through a lens of sadness for the person delivering the message—to turn the other cheek and have pity on their soul. But I also had to say something to an adult to ensure that people would be aware and things would change for future children. Remember, my brother and I were among the first set of children to desegregate Austin schools.

From preschool to first grade, I could just be myself while attending private St. Martin's Lutheran School. The children were used to me having the metal rods on my legs and the orthopedic shoes and did not make fun of me. But when my parents enrolled my brother and me at Pease Elementary, a public school, in my second-grade and his kindergarten year, I soon learned that a kid with allergies, orthopedic shoes, and leg braces would be treated very differently.

Upon reflection, after I started public school, I was often a sad child and developed a condition of nail biting until Mom found some awful-tasting nail polish. It was a time of being excluded, bullied, and almost killed (*more on that in the next chapter*)! We all know that kid with the Kleenex—that was me! Each day, my mom would tuck the pocket-sized packets of Kleenex into my lunch box, along with an extra one for my book bag.

There were students who tripped me and called my shoes "roach busters," who poured water on my braces to make them rust. One kid in particular took great glee in squealing in a high-pitched voice, "Rockin' Robin, squeak, squeak, squeak . . ." (to the Bobby Day tune) as I walked down the hall to make fun of the metallic sound of the braces. After a few weeks of this, I begged my parents to let me just wear the shoes to school and the braces at home and weekends. After the pediatrician signed off, they agreed, and the bullying got a little better.

Only after the kids discovered that my clunky shoes were perfect for kickball did the initial objection to having me on the team turn into my biggest advantage. I might not have been able to run fast, but I could kick the ball so far away. I was often the fourth kicker so that if there were full bases, everyone could run in and our team could win! Those shoes turned a negative into a positive, and allowed me to be among the first group of kids to be picked for a team.

The first time I wore real sneakers was in fourth grade: blue Nike LD-1000s. I was so excited, but the other kids did not know that my orthopedist had cut the shoes apart and placed a plaster arch support mold in the bottom of the shoe that would stabilize my foot. And as soon as I got in the car on the way home from school, I had to change into my orthopedic shoes and braces to start the work again as my legs and feet began to turn back in after those few hours.

My doctor said that when I entered puberty, that would be near the end of the braces and orthopedic shoes. I was already 5'8" in sixth grade, and he did not think that I would grow much more. When my growth plates connected, he was certain that I would be in the clear, but that meant that I needed strong muscles to support me.

My daily life consisted of kids making fun of me, getting good grades, Kleenex at my face, and medical trauma from weekly microdosing to build up my immunity. I spent so many hours in the doctor's office that he ordered a weekly Scholastic magazine subscription so that I would have something new to read while there. I had to wait there at least an hour after eating a potentially triggering item, treat any reaction, and then wait until it subsided, thus building up a tolerance threshold to be able to handle a little more in the future. Swinging my legs with squeaking metal braces. Week after week. Year after year.

In fact, some adults talked loud and slow when they saw my leg braces, as if my ears were broken. If they were too out of control, my mom would sometimes say, "Her ears aren't broken," and then embarrassment would register on their faces.

> My advice to anyone is: Never underestimate someone based on appearance. Their "disadvantage" or difference could be just what is needed to ultimately make your team a winner!

The summer before we went to public school, we were spending part of the summer with my maternal grandparents outside Houston. I was six and my brother was five. I probably asked, "What do you do all day?" So my grandfather decided to show us what he did by taking us to work with him. I remember eating a grown-up breakfast with him (toast and tea—he had coffee!), wearing a dress with white tights and saddle shoes that connected to my braces, and carrying a parasol. My brother wore his typical outfit of shorts and a polo-style shirt. I was rarely conscious of my leg braces in the country because people knew me from birth and respected my grandparents, so they never made any comments.

That morning, we rode in the nice pickup with Granddaddy to visit some of his properties. We went to a block that had plain, cottage-style houses called shotgun shacks. They were all due to be painted, and as we stepped out of the truck, my brother began to entertain himself by tossing white crushed seashells used on the driveways (much like pea gravel is used in the Northeast) in front of the houses up and down the block. My brother threw shells into the gulley drain and was oblivious to the worker activity on the street.

But Granddaddy and I stood side by side, and I used my parasol to shield my eyes from the glare of the Texas sun.

"So, Robin," said Granddaddy. "What color should we paint these houses?"

"Easter egg colors!" I chirped, barely giving it a thought.

"Easter egg colors it is then," he said as formally as if he was striking a deal with the workers assigned to do the work. The way he spoke to me was with respect and as though he cared about my opinion. He went up to the foreman and spoke to him, and then we hopped back in the truck.

A few days later, we drove down the block and saw the finished product. Imagine my delight at the transformation of real houses painted white with eaves, shutters, and doors in Easter egg pastel colors. This was real! No two houses were the same!

Before that moment, my life was one-dimensional with a coloring book. But now, my perspective changed to a three-dimensional awareness with real houses on a real street, with real people living in them! Something clicked inside me. This was what I wanted to do . . . but what was this called? Inside, my body was spinning. I remember tapping my shoes with my squeaking leg braces because I could not stay still. Wow! *I want to feel this again*, I thought.

This was the first time someone had cared about my opinion, and then actually acted upon it! As I almost started to bounce around from excitement, my grandfather told me to stand up properly and to remember that I was representing the family and our business. I heard the words "our business" and straightened my spine and mimicked his stance of crossed arms and a quiet look of observation.

Back in the truck, I told Granddaddy that I wanted to be a housepainter.

He sternly looked at me and said, "No. You can design them and select the colors, but you will not be climbing on a ladder. Those jobs are called architect, designer, or developer." At six years old, I heard him, and my subconscious heard him too.

From that point onward, Granddaddy wanted me to understand generational wealth, and I was a great student as a young girl. He often showed me around the real estate properties while collecting rents, painting, or renovating, or during each summer I worked at the general store.

Another blessing due to my allergies: My brother had to do hard labor (which he loved!) such as feeding pigs or cows, mucking horse stalls, fixing fence posts, or doing janitorial work. And I was typically in air conditioning due to allergic triggers, bugs, or odiferous farm smells!

Business and properties were physical marks of success for my mom's family, but it was the intangible success that was more important—the relationships. Granddaddy pointed out the men who worked for him: master carpenters, painters, framers, and ranch hands. Some for a few years; some for a decade or more. And some of their sons were now starting to work for him too.

He explained that there was probably better money to be found elsewhere, but he had fostered a culture of year-round job security, compassion, meals (he paid for a lunch truck many days), and discounts or credit at the general store for family groceries.

"Communication and transparency are everything," he said.

I observed this in the way he managed each job site, as busy as it was, with respect to all the workers. He would correct privately and praise publicly in a way that connoted respect. It was a well-oiled machine: a team. Opinions were heard and considered, even if not always acted upon—and he fostered a sense of respect for the expertise of these men.

And as his granddaughter, there was a certain level of respect that was as yet unearned, but visible in the deference I received as I got older.

Great Granddaddy was the first to start teaching me about money. Our routine would go something like this:

"Have you been a good little girl this week? Did you get any spankings?"

"Yes, Great Granddaddy. No, Great Granddaddy."

With the right answers, he would then reach into a pouch he always kept handy. Upturning it over the palm of his hand, out would tumble two silver dollars that he always called "big nickels."

"Here are two big nickels for you," he would solemnly announce. "One is for spending. The other is for saving."

Going to the bank in the company of Great Granddaddy or Granddaddy was always a dress-up occasion. A pretty dress. Patent leather shoes and ankle socks with lace. Sometimes white gloves or a parasol. He was teaching me that the family kept up appearances, and going to the bank was serious business. Money was to be respected and gained by work.

Spending three weeks with them in the summer was a learning experience. I learned about money by handling real currency, not Monopoly money. My first job was counting and rolling change into paper sleeves. Each day, heavy bags of change came from the laundromat, parking lots, or the general store cash register. It would take a while to count and put the change into the paper sleeves. And we (the cousins, my brother, and I) would put our initials on the side in crayon. The one who rolled the most got a quarter. That went quite far because Dubble Bubble gum was only a penny. And I won most of the time because the others would get distracted by cartoons.

When we went to the bank, we got a lollipop from the teller, and if the count was accurate, a paper dollar was added to our personal allowance tally for rolling the change accurately. I earned about $25 a week for a few hours of work at six years old, and 75 percent of that went into the bank for savings.

My memories of Great Granddaddy match the photos. He was an elegant, dapper man who always wore Brooks Brothers dress shirts and Borsalino hats, which he carefully protected in specially made hatboxes. I will always associate these hats with Great Granddaddy, and only fully understood how valuable they were after walking past the Fifth Avenue store in New York City decades later.

Great Granddaddy is the one who first explained the concept of "passing"—which he would do while conducting business in Houston. But he always emphasized that he returned to the country to live his authentic life—returning to his family of many shades—due to his three marriages, and each woman having a different shade of skin from fair to nut brown.

Independent even into his extreme old age, Great Granddaddy lived in a carriage house behind Granny and his son, Robert Scott. He enjoyed living on his own, with the regular cadence of them bringing him meals (always knock first) that he called "room service." I still remember the smell of the pipe tobacco and Cuban cigars that nestled deep within his clothing, but he would never smoke around me because of my "constitution," as he called it.

Great Granddaddy was fit and robust, even though he smoked a pipe and smelled of expensive cigars, which he referred to as "my Cubans." Given that importing Cuban cigars was illegal in the 1970s, I am going to assume that he legally sourced them, and I recall that they were the Montecristo brand. Realistically, I'm still wondering if he got them from the sailors on ships docked at the Galveston port, or if they were legally imported from the Dominican Republic, where they were also made by Cuban exiles.

With his own space, which allowed him to smoke pipes and cigars, he also played jazz records on his ancient Victrola, often loud enough to drown out the sounds of the PTL religious channel coming from the TV in his daughter-in-law's living room. When we visited the "country," all the grandkids would sit in his cottage behind the main house to listen to music played on his Victrola—typically jazz or blues music by Count Basie, Robert Johnson, Ma Rainey, John Coltrane, Bessie Smith, or Louis Armstrong.

Great Granddaddy was a Christian, but he believed that for some, the church building was actually a hospital for sinners. He despised religious hypocrites who "started sinning on Friday, hurt their wives on Saturday, and kept up appearances on Sunday in the front pews with bloodshot eyes and bloodied knuckles." He said that "real church" was how you behaved daily toward others and the unseen good deeds done for those who could do nothing for you. He always reminded the grandkids that actions will always speak louder than words.

On my dad's side of the family, my Grandpapa remained connected to the land by managing a small backyard garden with a hand plow. He was an alchemist with his fertilizer mixtures, and he explained the importance of bees and earthworms to the ecosystem, and showed us how insects, earthworms, and pollen helped his garden and the organic food on our table.

He taught me about growing farm-to-table produce like snap peas, carrots, lettuce, cabbage, tomatoes, peas, and cucumbers, which supplemented store-bought food. He also had apple, pear, and fig trees. My horror was bugs, bees, and earthworms, but these filled my brother with glee.

Due to a lifetime of hard work, both my paternal grandparents were afflicted with many physical ailments as they aged. Grandpapa had worked to build the railroad across the state when the cotton harvest was done, so his arm muscles were huge, but he had back issues, difficulty walking or sitting in comfort, and often slept in a recliner. Grandmother had back issues and pains from birthing ten children, along with years of sewing and housekeeping.

Grandpapa died when I was seven, and my few memories of him are about his love of farming and his love for his grandchildren. Grandmother died when I was in college, but before her dementia, she taught me the art of folding fitted sheets, quilting, cooking, baking, making preserves, and her secret cleaning recipes with toothpaste, vinegar, lemon juice, and Coca-Cola.

Upon reflection, this was a time when I was developing a root system, a treasure chest of wisdom from all the people who planted knowledge and thoughts in my psyche so that I would understand reasons for a strong work ethic. Watching my grandfather treat workers with dignity guides my moral and ethical compass today—sometimes I give too many chances to team members, but I am rarely inclined to fire on the first offense. It's helped my decision-making for a lifetime of entrepreneurship.

And knowing that my parents sacrificed years of their life to work with a pediatrician to build me into a healthy child, *so that I could have an even healthier adult life*, makes me so grateful. It reminds me of this metaphor: "Your reality is directly correlated to your goals, and your comfort with the inverse." For example, eating a well-balanced diet today may not be comfortable or easy at times, but in the future, you will be much healthier and more comfortable.

A sacrifice today can make all the difference tomorrow!

It is my belief that we all know what we want to do—what will make us happy—before the age of seven (a time before the "bugs" of peer pressure can change our direction!). Often, somewhere along the way, with other opinions or a "declare your major" moment, we change our minds and ignore what makes us happy.

Just remember that if you have an opportunity to do your calling, you will love what you do, and as some would say: "You will never work a day in your life." If you have an opportunity to do "that thing," you should try to move in that direction.

QUESTIONS TO COMB THROUGH

1. Are there any genetic commonalities in your family—allergies, a need for braces, eyeglasses?
2. Is bullying something that you experienced or witnessed (and did not intervene in), or that you participated in and you look back on with regret? What do you need to "comb out"?
3. When you reflect on your childhood, did you know what you wanted to do when you were between ages four and six, and does any element of your career reflect your vision?

Chapter 3

LEAVES

When a cotton plant establishes itself, it develops leaves and root systems that begin to grow more extensively. At this stage, the plant is vulnerable to disease and pests and needs protection.

I remember my first racist incident in preschool, between the ages of four and five. A boy put his arm next to mine, as if to compare them, and asked me why I was dirty. He said he couldn't play with me because I didn't belong at the school, then called me the N-word. I cried because of his tone, not fully understanding the boy's words but feeling his hatred and realizing he'd made me self-conscious of something that I could not change.

Tragically, that night, I tried to get the dirt off in the bath—picking up the Brillo pad used to clean the tub and attempting to rub my skin. My mom came into the bathroom when she didn't hear my typical happy singing and looked at the raw skin on my arms in horror. She shrieked and asked me what I was doing. "Baby, what in the world?"

I told her about my school experience that day and asked her how I could get clean. "Mama, this dirt. It won't come off. I want it off," I cried.

"Robin, stop it. You cannot remove your skin. You are unique. That is part of who you are. Your color is not what you are, but a part of who you are. You are beautiful. And always remember that your skin color is your superpower! Whenever you enter a room, people will notice you—they will remember you. You might be the only chocolate chip in the sea of vanilla, but everyone will remember you because you are one-of-one. Your father and I will speak to the teacher in the morning, but right now, we need to bandage your skin. Oh baby . . ."

The next day, both Mom and Dad came with me to preschool, and they did not just drive away. They dropped me off in the classroom and stayed to meet with the teacher and principal. I wore a long-sleeved shirt that covered up bandages. Remember that my brother and I were among the first Black kids to desegregate our private school in 1973.

At some point, the teacher called the boy out of the room. I never saw him again and learned years later that when his parents arrived and learned about the incident, they decided to transfer him to another school. No apology, no teaching their child, just running away from the fact that they likely spoke that way in their home.

But I am left with the words from my parents: *Your difference is a superpower!*

"Eat it!" the teacher hissed.

It was my second week in second grade at my new school, Pease Elementary—the oldest public elementary school in the state of Texas. Mrs. Black, my classroom teacher, was assigned lunch monitor duties. She was obviously from the Clean Your Plate Club (CYPC).

"I said eat your food. There are starving children in Africa," she roared as she leaned over me. Her screeching tone made the cafeteria silent, and it felt like all heads turned on a swivel to look at the new girl receiving the wrath of gray-haired, red-lipped Mrs. Black.

I have tried to remember how she intimidated me into doing the one thing I knew that I should never do. What I do know is that somewhere in the school nurse's office, there was a file with my name on it that advised everyone who bothered to look that this child was pan-allergic to certain foods.

Meekly, I squeaked, "I'm allergic to dairy and can't eat that. Please call my mom." Growing up sickly and pan-allergic in a state where everything is supersized, I was taught by my mom and pediatrician to develop an all-hazards approach to certain foods. I kept my hands in my lap and did not reach for the food.

Mom normally packed my lunch, but on this day, I had begged her for money to pay for school lunch so I could fit in. The menu was supposed to have been a chicken dish, but instead they substituted a grilled cheese sandwich. Moving down the cafeteria line, the selection was a grilled cheese sandwich, tater tots, ketchup, a choice of fruit, and milk.

I ate the tater tots from my multi-divider plate, covering

them with ketchup, and took a bite of my apple, leaving everything else.

"Please call my mom," I weakly repeated, still staring down at my lap because I couldn't stand her eyes staring at me. The last thing I wanted to do was continue to make a scene and draw more attention to myself. As my eyes darted, I noticed the Black custodian looking at me, standing in the corner. He stood still, staring at the scene, resting on his mop in his gray khakis.

"Oh, she's going to hear from me, alright, about your smart-aleck mouth," Mrs. Black hissed. "Eat what's on your plate. You are just a picky eater. Stop being stubborn."

I was only six years old, and one of the few Black students in the newly integrated Pease Elementary School. She bent at the waist, lowered her head to meet my eyes, and started wagging her finger. I didn't dare look up and go eye to eye with this grown-up.

I looked back at the plate, trying to find a way to avoid eating that grilled cheese sandwich. Congealed on white bread. Fake bread, not whole wheat. Fluorescent orange like a melted tangerine crayon. I did not know what to do, and this war of wills made other kids put down their sandwiches to see the new girl being humiliated—and to see if my defiance would last. I could almost see the kids willing me to eat the sandwich. In my mind, I just wanted it to be over . . . A tiny bite wouldn't hurt, right?

"*Eat it!*" came the demand again with a snarl.

I reached sloth-like toward the slab of sandwich and thought, *Well, maybe just a teeny bit.* I could fake it by lifting a corner of it to my lips and politely saying, "Mmmm, delicious." Maybe even smile a little bit.

I took that bite. And then I almost died. I knew that the small bite was a big mistake.

Within seconds, my body went into anaphylactic shock. My friends told me later that my eyes had bulged like a frog, and I had started to breathe funny. I grabbed my throat and tried to stand up but collapsed at the feet of Mrs. Black. She stared and then screamed at me to get up. Then she screamed for help when I started to gag. I heard the kids murmuring and was embarrassed but could not breathe.

The custodian ran and picked up my limp body, carrying me up the stairs to the nurse's office. I remember the sound of his keys or change jangling, and that he screamed when he entered the office. Then it went black.

Maybe I cried. Maybe I didn't. I don't remember too much. I guess there was a phone call to my mother somewhere in that short timeline. I think the principal rode in the ambulance with me.

I vaguely remember being strapped onto a gurney with kids watching through the school windows, then being wheeled into an ambulance, the wailing of a siren, and the bouncing during the ambulance ride to the hospital. The nurses at Brackenridge Hospital knew me, and the nice one with blond hair held my hand, but she looked worried. She was always so nice when I came into the hospital with an asthma attack, but this time she was not smiling. This was something else.

Time was weird. I would open my eyes and see daylight, and then it would be night. I remember seeing the hazy faces of my pediatrician and my mom, but it was confusing, and I mostly remember black—nothingness, peacefulness, sleep. I was not scared, but kept hearing voices that sounded far away: my mom, my dad, a doctor, a nurse.

When I hear others speak today about being at that point where they have to make a choice between life or just resting forever in the peacefulness of the black, I know what they're talking about. Sometime during that period, the decision was made to take out my tonsils. When I awoke a few days later, there was great pain in my throat. My mom told me that at one point, I actually fell out of the bed because a nurse forgot to put the railing up. She said that I bounced and never woke up. Mom was sleeping in my room on a cot and jumped as all the nurses came running when they heard the thud. She said that they just put me back in bed because I never woke up.

Most kids get ice cream when their tonsils are removed. I remember watching my parents eating my ice cream in my hospital room.

Me? I could only have JELL-O or crushed ice because I was allergic to dairy.

What about that teacher? All I know is this: She shouted me into the hospital.

Had she read a book on child psychology and unilaterally diagnosed my behavior as *attention-getting* and chosen to embarrass me into submission? Was she resentful of the desegregation of the new brown faces in my school? There is no telling for sure, really.

When I went back to school, my principal transferred me out of Mrs. Black's classroom to another teacher's class. Whenever I saw her, she would try to be nice, but let's face it, she almost killed me!

I never saw her as a lunch monitor again in the school cafeteria, and there was never a CYPC moment again, as my mom volunteered for lunch duty to make sure that I always had a Tupperware with my lunch in it.

Looking back: Had it not been for three adults who acted quickly—the custodian, the nurse, and the principal—I might not have grown up or seen my family again.

As an adult, the reality hit me: I could have died.

There were plenty of people who didn't believe in allergies and thought my mom was exaggerating, but we knew what one bite could do . . . and I did not want to go back to the blackness again. Even relatives tried to tempt me with ice cream, pizza, or other snack foods. But anyone who knew about "the incident" was clear about the consequences and would stop the adult or child from trying to convince me to eat a forbidden item.

Hawaiian Punch. Tang. Kool-Aid. Hi-C. Orange Crush. Big Red. Those were the drinks that other kids had in their lunch boxes. I had water.

Froot Loops. Cap'n Crunch. Frosted Flakes. Cocoa Krispies. Trix. Lucky Charms. Those were cereals the other kids and my brother ate for breakfast with milk. I had Cheerios and water.

Yes, water! Water. Water. Water. Sometimes with a slice of lemon, but most of the time plain.

My mom says it was like this:

> As far as what she could drink was concerned, Robin could only have water. She certainly couldn't have the canned fruit juices and punches her friends had at their birthday parties. And she couldn't even have milk on her cereal. It could only be water. The doctor was trying to reset her system, and he needed to know what she ingested.
>
> Her brother, Russel, was born about fourteen months

after Robin. He would tease her by making a big show out of enjoying all the foods he ate. Things she could not have—basics of childhood like ice cream, pizza, mac and cheese, or milk on his cereal.

And Robin would sit there in tears or leave the table. Luckily, they ended up close as they grew up. Child birthday parties were so hard due to her allergies. She had to bring her Tupperware to the parties, or we had to turn down the invitations to her friends' events held at their homes due to the presence of furry pets. So, we often packed her red Tupperware with her snack, or she would give a present, stay for fun activities, and we would leave before cake or ice cream. So, after a time, they stopped inviting her. It was quite painful. Even her birthday party was hard to handle. One year, we just rented the go-kart track, but Robin could not even eat the pizza, or her own birthday cake, or ice cream. She just couldn't tolerate it, so she cried on her birthday.

Over time, her food tolerances grew, and as an adult she knows her limit when she does have those foods. She describes it as a scratchy feeling in her throat, and she will stop eating.

I remember one time when our family bought tickets to the Barnum & Bailey Circus. My brother and I were so excited to see elephants and other wild animals. When we parked and the car door opened, I felt that tickle but thought it was from the dust in the air. And then we got closer to the tent and the animals were outside, and I started to feel the tightness in my throat and my ears started to feel pressure. My mom glanced at me and saw me rub my ears and nose. I remember saying, "I'm okay," as we entered the tent.

We made it through the acrobatics, but by this time, I was mouth breathing. We saw the animals parade in, and by that time, I felt my eyes swelling. And then my parents looked at me, and they picked me up and we rushed out—straight to the hospital. I had broken out into hives, and my eyes were starting to bulge and close. My brother was upset because he wanted to stay, and I just concentrated on trying to breathe calmly.

The doctor indicated that the animal dander, dust, and sensitivity caused multiple reactions just by coming into the circus tent filled with several allergic triggers. The easiest way to describe an asthma attack is: *You are choking air in, but you cannot breathe it out*. And then there is no room left to even breathe in. And hives feel like thousands of ant stings, but they don't itch as much as burn. The physical toll on my body was a constant stress reaction, and I was already very thin due to the diet limitations and my height. My reality was just trying to stay alive, and after this incident, my doctor said that we needed to work on getting my lungs stronger. And since he planned to remove my leg brace requirement after fourth grade, he wanted me to start an exercise program.

Swimming did not work because I could not hold my breath very long, and my hair was a mess after swimming in a chlorine pool. I tried tennis but could not stabilize my legs and feet initially. So, Mom made me walk a high school track daily for two laps. And my parents bought three-speed bikes for me and my brother.

A year later in fifth grade, I started track. By eighth grade, I joined the track team and became a sprinter, running the 220-, 440-, and 880-meter races. Track was not something I could sustain, and in my last race, I collapsed on the track after crossing the finish line and had to be treated for an asthma attack. Once again, embarrassment in front of my classmates. That ended my track career, but my legs were stronger after three years of training, and tennis later became my sport!

Says my mom:

> People don't understand that when you start out centered, you are likely to stay that way. People may have a color, an accent, a hometown that is different. But everyone has an inner self. Once you know who your inner person is, you choose to be a good or a bad person—and decide to have a good or a bad day. But ultimately, you decide, because it's you . . . God put you on earth to teach both you and others something. Just be *you*.

Looking back on this phase of my life, my parents were and are my heroes. With a limited budget, they found a way to keep me protected with a holistic pediatrician. Their actions were my first model of what miracles can be accomplished when we seek out the best advice from the wisest resources and the positive results that are possible when we act on that advice.

Many of my life's turning points began with someone who cared enough to say, "You might want to pay attention to this crossroad coming up." My mother was the start of it all—always making sure it was safe to enter an intersection by making good choices. Dad was there to back her up and be a calming force in any storm. Together, their partnership established a root system that protected me from the CYPC mindset and the ability to say no to anyone who tried to tempt me with things that were not good for me!

Questions to Comb Through

1. Have you ever been in a situation where someone tried to make you do something that you knew you should not? How did you handle that moment?
2. If you had to wear something that might identify you as differently abled, do you think you might have more compassion for others? Do you pause to hold open the door for the person with a wheelchair, crutches, or leg braces?
3. Do you understand that certain allergies can kill people? If someone says they do not want to eat something or be in a certain space due to an allergy, do you keep insisting?

Chapter 4

FLOWERING

The cotton plant produces flowers that develop into bolls, which go through three stages: growth, filling, and maturation. The bolls split open at maturity after 140–160 days to reveal the white cotton fibers inside—this is often called the "white field" stage. When open, the bolls are ready for harvesting.

"Move to the back row," said my sixth-grade schoolteacher. I complied, standing eye to eye with her as a ten-year-old. It was school picture day, and the tallest kids went to the back of the bleachers. At 5'8" and ninety-nine pounds, my new nickname was Olive Oyl—the lanky character in the Popeye cartoons. My mother always found a silver lining by telling me that she was proud that I was the only one who was not slouching compared to some others in the back row.

Thin, tall, and awkward is how I would describe myself at that age. Getting used to the lightweight Nike sneakers (compared to the leather orthopedic shoes with the plaster cast inside) was a challenge, so I walked in a unique prance to compensate. Teachers at my school knew about the incident in second grade, so on bad pollen days, I stayed inside, tidied up the classroom, graded other students' papers, and was allowed to read in the library in the bean bag chairs.

By the time I entered sixth grade, the after-school program allowed me to be a teacher's assistant, helping with hanging younger-grade art projects in the hallways and tutoring—all kinds of tasks, except for clapping chalk erasers due to my allergies. Awkwardly, at the sixth-grade graduation, the librarian gave me an award for reading the most books in the school!

In middle school, I was the editor of the school newspaper, and my parents invested in a personal computer with dial-up service. Most of the time, the computer was used as a word processor, and the guest room was set up as a study with bookcases, a daybed, and a computer desk where my brother and I could do our homework.

We had moved from East Austin in fifth grade and now lived in a new house near the Arboretum in Northwest Austin. Instead of going to the neighborhood school, my parents allowed me to transfer to my original school so I would keep the same friends. Each day, my brother and I were driven to O. Henry Middle School or Pease Elementary, which was a twelve-mile drive each way. And each campus was near my mother's job (in case there was a health situation).

She was a helicopter parent before there was such a term and made the most of being a PTA mom and class mom, and she volunteered in the attendance office and helped fundraise for the school at events. Regularly, the other kids would say, "Your mom is here," so I was always on my best behavior. Other kids were socializing, behaving badly, and managing social norms, and I was just trying to navigate as an academically gifted, yet personally awkward, tween—and my path was limited as my mom was always ready to swoop in.

At the time, I resented her visibility but recognize her concern (today in my role as a parent!) was born of almost losing her daughter due to a CYPC teacher years earlier. And when I learned later what some of my classmates were doing as early as junior high, I am grateful that my path was not set in that direction.

At both O. Henry Middle School and S.F. Austin High School, there were some kids from my old East Austin neighborhood who were bused in. Wealthier kids from Tarrytown and Clarksville were driven by their parents, drove their own cars, or rode the bus. I was driven to school daily. Since we now lived in Northwest Austin, it felt like I lived on an island because I had never attended school with kids in my neighborhood.

Color lines and class lines exist within all communities. They are, as W. E. B. Du Bois wrote, ". . . as separate as the five fingers, and yet one as the hand in all things essential to mutual progress." Our true character is not about the words we say, but in the thoughts we think privately and the actions we deliver publicly.

Many of the Black kids labeled smart kids like me as "Oreo," "bougie," or "wanting to be white" because we spoke well, studied hard, and joined student organizations. It was challenging to just "be myself," which was the mantra said daily by my mom.

One bully threatened me one day because I would not give him a hint at the test questions for a class that I had just taken. I don't remember what he said, but I put him in his place when I said, "My dad knew your dad in high school." His shocked look stopped him in his tracks, and he shrank back and slunk away. From that point forward, I was never bullied again by him or his crowd.

The reason: He barely knew his father. And now he knew that I knew why. His father was in prison. His toughness may have been the shield to protect him at school, but at the end of the day, he was just a kid in pain. A few days later, he asked if he could speak to my dad during school pickup. I asked my dad and he said, "Of course." A few days later, this guy had finished sports practice and was waiting for the school bus to take him home, and Dad drove up.

For about thirty minutes, my dad took the time to speak to him about his memories of his father in high school—and it was one of the few times that I saw the bully soften because he had never heard the stories or learned about his dad from "before" his situation. My dad simply told him to do his best and not to follow the same path. The boy changed a bit after that talk and began to study harder instead of solely focusing on sports.

I had "protection" from the other bullies for the rest of my school years. My dad often said that boys without a father in their home need to hear words of wisdom from other men, who will guide them to make good choices. And that boy ended up graduating on time.

I was thirteen and in high school when a woman who looked like Jennifer Grey with straight hair stared in my direction at the Safeway grocery across the frozen vegetables. I thought she was looking at me because she was concerned that there was no adult around. But finally, this woman said these magical words to me: "Are you a model?"

I turned around to see who she was talking to, but there was no one behind me. She was talking to me! I could feel her focus on me like heat across the frozen air, and I realized she really meant it.

"I'm not, but I do watch the Elsa Klensch Style Show on CNN," I responded. "It looks like fun."

"Where is your mom?" she asked. I pointed to the parking lot. She handed me her card, which I put in my Girbaud jeans pocket, and then she said the magical words: "I'm a model scout and own an agency. I'm coming out to meet your mom, and I hope we can sign you and work together." Her tone was so confident, and I was mesmerized.

Her agency was BLVD, and her name was Debbi Branda. At that time, it was the top modeling agency in Austin. I later learned that she had worked in New York City as a scout for the top agencies. In fact, one of my classmates at Austin High, who regularly appeared in the Style section of the newspaper and in fashion shows, was represented by this agency.

Debbi abandoned her cart and waited with me while I checked out. My hands were shaking due to excitement, and I may have dropped the change. I made sure to be polite and say thank you to the cashier. I carefully held the brown paper bag, receipt, and change for my mother—as I held my head high and tried to walk with perfect posture to our 1976 Oldsmobile Cutlass Vista Cruiser station wagon with tan top, wood panel decal, and wire hubcaps.

As I walked out of the Safeway with a white lady by my side, my mother swiveled her head and narrowed her eyes. I knew that look and began to tremble inside, knowing that she thought that I had done something bad, like shoplifting, requiring an adult to escort me out of the market. She was also embarrassed because she was wearing a house dress and her hair was in curlers—hence the reason for my running an errand in the store by myself.

"Mom, this lady wants to talk to you," I started to say.

"Get. In. The. Car," she hissed, and I swear her lips did not move as her eyes narrowed further. Then she swiveled her head and turned on the charm for the lady with a smile and a look of concern. I slid into the passenger seat with a paper bag of Blue Bell ice cream, frozen vegetables, and juice concentrate resting on my lap.

"Mom, this is a good thing! Just listen to her!" I stage whispered.

My mother swiveled her head and looked at me. If she had been a cobra, I would be dead. I knew that another word out of my mouth would mean . . .

The woman started talking. "My name is Debbi Branda, and I run the BLVD Modeling Agency. Your daughter is beautiful, and she told me that she is only thirteen, so I wanted to meet you and tell you that she should consider modeling. She is so thin and tall for her age. We are looking for new faces, and she could be someone we want to represent. I think your daughter has what it takes to potentially be a model. And I would love to chat with you about that."

My mother responded predictably, like most parents, as she accepted the business card. "Okay, thank you. I'll speak to my husband. Have a great evening. Bye."

Debbi walked away as the driver's side power window rolled up. My mother glared at me again and muttered, "I have told you not to speak to strangers." She put the car in gear, and we drove home with an awkward silence between us on the brown bench seat. I fingered the business card in my jeans pocket.

What I remember most is that this was the first time someone outside my family had called me beautiful—and it made me feel special. I think that I saw a shooting star when I looked out the windshield.

When we got home, I was unpacking the groceries when she brought it up to my dad. My brother was watching TV and he just fell onto his side and started guffawing. Feelings hurt, I went to my room and secretly stashed the business card that Debbi had given me. I hid it in my music box to make sure that it did not get washed in the laundry. Now my music box held a treasure!

I started to visualize my new identity and practiced smiling, posing for photos, and walking on the runway. This meant a regular viewing of the CNN show *Style with Elsa Klensch,* and admiring the walks of the supermodels who strutted down the catwalk or in ads known only by first name: Naomi, Gail, Linda, Veronica, Christy, Tatjana, Cindy, and Paulina. They were all so unique and beautiful!

Around this time, I became like most teenagers—pushing my mom away even though I knew her caring and watchful actions were about keeping me healthy. My identity was forming, and my dreams were too big for my hometown. All the traits that modeling loved—too thin, too tall, unique walk, long neck, perfect posture—were things that I loathed, but I would soon learn that my "look" would work to my benefit.

And I dreamt of any self-definition other than a sickly, pan-allergic child. It was about having a new perspective. Debbi and BLVD became the connector to help me visualize for my future—and a chance to be something in the bigger world. She actually saw me, and these new opportunities would help pave the way to my future. As Mom said, being "me" was enough!

During my next school day, I asked my friend about Debbi, and she said, "She is the greatest. All my photo shoots with Dillard's and runway work are through BLVD. I am saving a lot of money for college." With that endorsement for college funds, I was sold. But I had to wait for the right moment to bring it up again with my parents.

I was Obedient Robin. Academic Robin. Allergic Robin. Braced-Leg Robin. But now I was determined to become Robin the Runway Model. But first the work began with mimicking high heels while watching the CNN Style show, practicing in the living room on tippy toes. Walking back and forth and copying the poses and turns from the runway. Trying to figure out a natural stride in a few feet. Trying to understand how to turn out without falling over. Trying to understand how to open a coat, take it off, and not stop. Trying to figure out a natural stride after years of orthopedic shoes and braces—building muscles for high heels without the shoes (for now!).

The work also included riding my bike, taking a dance class to learn about my body movements, and starting to eat less and even healthier. I was already skinny. I got skinnier. I subscribed to *Vogue*, *W*, *Glamour*, *Mademoiselle*, and *Newsweek* magazines. I used one of those Publishers Clearing House coupons to get five subscriptions for a dollar (or some otherwise ridiculously small amount of money).

At the next checkup, my pediatrician asked me if I was anorexic or bulimic. I didn't know what either was, but I did know that I was skipping meals. No one told me to do so, but I saw how skinny the models were. Then someone said it out loud on one of the TV shows: ". . . a model's job is to be a hanger for the clothes."

I'd never really thought about fashion before, but I began to coordinate outfits differently, studying photos, poses, and trends in the magazine pages. When magazines arrived, the perfume cards were thrown out, as they triggered wheezing. I learned the first names of all the top designers, bopped to George Michael's music, and obsessed about the way models walked: tall girls with great posture and S-curve catwalk poses. I created an exaggerated walk since my legs were still slightly curved, even after many years with braces. There was no makeup because Mom did not wear it. So, I had to imagine.

Only a few months until my fourteenth birthday.

A few days before my fourteenth birthday was the right moment. My parents offhandedly said that I could "do anything" for my birthday. "Anything?" I checked. Mom nodded. Here was my chance.

"Okay, I know what I want. Can we call and meet Debbi Branda?" I instantly answered.

"Who?" my parents said in unison.

"You know, that model scout lady. The agent. We met her at the Safeway last year," I replied. "She gave you her business card."

"Oh. I lost that card ages ago," my mother deflected. "What else would you like to do instead?"

"Oh, she gave me her card too. I have it—let me go get it," I replied and ran up the stairs. I had memorized her number, even if Mom had thrown this one away. I bounded back downstairs, and my parents looked at each other. I think my dad gulped.

"Okay . . . what do you want us to do?" my parents asked.

"Call her and schedule a meeting." My dad put his head in his hands. My mom looked at me with a perplexed look. But they had promised. She picked up the brown wall phone in the kitchen with the extra-long cord.

"Hello, this is Robin Wilson's mother. You met my daughter at Safeway last year. She turns fourteen in a few days, and for her birthday present, she has asked to meet with you. I don't know if you remember her?"

Debbi was so happy to hear from us. "Yes! Of course, I remember. One of the models on our team told me that she goes to school with Robin." My mom actually admired that girl, who was from a well-respected family, one of the top students, and a cheerleader at Austin High. Mom raised her eyebrow, and I knew that Debbi had passed the first test from her expression.

"Before we talk about modeling and what might be Robin's future," Debbi suggested, "why don't you both come to the opening of Koala Blue at The Arboretum on Saturday? It is the new Olivia Newton-John swimwear store, and you will get front-row seats. And we can talk after the show?"

She continued, "That way you can see what we do. And Robin's classmate is booked for that show. Look forward to seeing you there, and afterward, we can have lunch and talk it over."

A few days later, we watched the show. Later at TGI Fridays, while Debbi and Mom talked, I ate calamari. "How much does it cost?" my mother asked.

"About $100 for headshots and a comp card, but we do not have fees because we are a real agency. Our job is to get talent booked for TV, print, or runway. We take 15 percent of their net. She will need some heels so she can learn to walk, a photo shoot, a beginner pack of makeup so she can practice, plus a nice black bag to carry everything in. Checks are issued within five days of receipt of the client payment," said Debbi.

Mom wrinkled her forehead. She knew there must be a catch somewhere.

Debbi continued, "Oh, and she has to take three classes, $50 per class. She has to learn how to walk, how to pose, and we do a class about how to handle a go-see booking, safety, and understanding call sheets. The class fees can be taken out of her first three bookings. I know that she will be booked based on her look. Our goal is to get work for talent. This is the real deal. Our talent gets booked in movies, commercials, fashion shows, and print throughout Texas and other states. And I or a colleague am on set for almost all shows and events to protect the girls."

"What else?" asked my mom.

"She should have a few things in her bag that are required, like a little mesh bag that models use to slip over their faces before they get dressed to protect garments from makeup, pantyhose in two shades: nude and black. But all the things will be on a call sheet before the booking. And you will always be able to call me," Debbi replied.

My mother turned to me. "I'll drive you to wherever you need to go for this activity," she said. "But you'll have to pay for all these things yourself, if you want it badly enough." My mom almost smirked because the numbers totaled over $300, and she thought that would buy her a few years!

But her expression was stunned when I said, "No problem. I have my babysitting money saved up. I want to do this! But I have one question. How much money did the models make for the show this morning?"

Debbi responded, "$700 for forty-two minutes walking the show."

I couldn't hold my excitement in. I exclaimed, "That's $3,500 for just five shows! I could buy a Hyundai for that!" My mother grimaced.

Debbi continued by saying this was a job, not just fun. She warned me that I still had to show up on time, be ready to work, and learn how to be talent. Her mantra was always, *"If you are on time, you are late."*

She reminded me that sometimes there would be rejection, and that I would just have to be ready to show up at every go-see with positive energy and good comportment.

Looking back at this moment, I realize that this was the first time that leveraging capital could propel me to the next major step up in life. Turning babysitting money into a modeling start-up fund for heels, makeup, workshops, and photo shoots allowed me to transform my income potential.

Rejection did not come frequently due to my all-American look, and I was booked for many shows, allowing me to earn enough for a down payment on a house in the first year. My first booking was a Dillard's holiday fashion show—with my parents in the front row, and my brother trying to make me laugh with his goofy faces. Very quickly, with the magic of makeup, hair, and posture, my young teenage self was cat-walking down runways all over Texas, wearing very grown-up fashions by haute couture designers at events produced by Saks Fifth Avenue, Scarbroughs, and Neiman Marcus. We also met several designers in person such as Mary McFadden, Todd Oldham, and Karl Lagerfeld.

One time, a panther was involved in a show, and I had to take medicine in advance due to my allergies. Dressed in a simple slip dress gown, I barely stayed on my feet while the panther hauled me forward toward the treat held by the handler at the end of the runway. There, I carefully made the turn as instructed, keeping the panther on a certain side as it had been trained.

Within seconds, I was propelled back down the runway, where another treat was waiting backstage. Then, the panther was placed in the kennel as we all sighed with relief and turned to walk the runway finale. That show paid $5,000, and my mom beamed from the audience as she saw my college fund growing!

I was booked by Doe Bailey to do a six-day set of shows for Saks Fifth Avenue in Monterrey, Guadalajara, and Mexico City. We carried number cards, and wealthy ladies bought couture designs in every color! More than once, I heard ladies in the front row say, "I wish I had that figure. What I wouldn't give for that waist."

That was my first introduction to the concept of appearance and illusion, and how an image can be used to sell an impossible dream. I would think to myself: *You are beautiful, and you have had children. This is a teenager's body you're looking at.*

We were strictly chaperoned as minors and had to be accompanied when we were not sequestered in our luxury hotel rooms. One day in Mexico City, we went to the mercado and piled five of us into a Volkswagen Beetle cab. Our guide was clear about which areas to avoid and how to negotiate. We tried to blend in, but that was impossible for a group of almost six-foot-tall girls. We thought we were blending in and just smiled a lot. We were absolutely clueless, but we made a lot of money for a few hours of work each day—and I remember studying for an exam when in my room so I could take it upon my return to school!

In haute couture, the smallest details matter: the finished seam, the hand stitching, small chains tucked into hems to ensure jackets hang perfectly, the distinct weave of fabrics, and the hours of craftsmanship. These garments taught me quality over quantity, and I began to prefer a few well-made garments rather than a closetful of disposable fashion.

Debbi was a stickler for time. She reminded us that when we were cast for a booking, we were responsible for being on time as the cast, crew, and client depended on us for a stress-free event, and they always wanted to limit production costs. Thousands of dollars were invested in even the smallest, most modest of shows. Debbi repeatedly warned us that being the model who caused everyone to worry, "Where is she?" was the model whose career was rapidly coming to an end. She taught us to be ten minutes early for everything. Today, I keep my car clock set a few minutes ahead so that I always arrive on time.

Modeling taught me so many other valuable life lessons, including how to enter a room: to pause and take in the scene before you fully commit to joining (i.e., read the room). Register your presence and thank the host. If it is not a room that you need to be in, walk around the perimeter, register a hello to the host, and walk right back out.

Even though the girls my age were beginning to experiment with makeup and wear it to school, I never wore makeup outside of my modeling work. I went fresh-faced everywhere because "your skin needs to breathe," Debbi would say. And then she would add, "Makeup can fix many flaws, but don't make it have to work so hard. Get your rest. Drink water."

I also learned to never look at myself in the mirror once dressed in the garment to be modeled. True, there would be full-length mirrors. But they were leaning against the wall at an angle, so we could see the clothing on our bodies but not our own faces. Our heads would be cut off at the top of the mirror frame. This way, we couldn't see *ourselves* in the designs.

Wearing that garment meant that I had to disappear, and my job was to breathe life and personality into the clothing, or at least be the character who would normally wear such an ensemble. So if I were wearing a Tina Turner–type dress, for example, I needed to walk on that runway to make those little beads and fringe trims swish around through movement. By contrast, if I were wearing a Chanel suit, I needed to walk a different way. None of those characters was me in real life. But it was fun to try them on for the length of the runway and back.

To my parents' immense credit, they did not allow me to have access to all my money between the ages of fourteen and twenty-one. They gave me a small allowance from those talent earnings and socked the rest away in an account I could access later in life. At the time, I was very upset and remember saying, "It's my money!"

But, decades later, I remain grateful that they did not let me blow it on the BMW 635i convertible that I wanted to buy myself for my sixteenth birthday. Instead, my parents bought me a used burnt-orange four-door Toyota Corolla from a rental car company with 40,000 miles on it for the commute to and from school. And funds were locked away for a future me. Lesson learned: Always think about how your future self will appreciate the frugality of today.

My main job was to be a good student and student leader. If I did not keep up my grades, the modeling would stop—and A's were the only acceptable choice. In my junior year of high school, I ran for student body president and won a term over a senior! What I learned from that election is that you must speak to a lot of people that may not be in your circle, as they want to hear what you will try to do for their issue. My opponent only spoke to his circle and did not work to reach different constituents. I remember going to the kids who viewed themselves as the "outcasts," and they were surprised that I wanted to know what they wanted to see change at the school. One of the important issues to that group was that the photography lab and video/audio departments be maintained so that they could express themselves. When I got elected, we lobbied for that funding, and the school found the money to continue those programs!

Leadership starts early, and it was challenging to cajole my classmates to arrive thirty minutes early to school for meetings, but they came when they learned that we would have snacks, attendance records would be shared, and they could get extra credit. We had a full semester of activities and were able to communicate with the administration about the "wish list" from the students. Our student leadership won some concessions, but what we all learned is that compromise is essential so that both sides feel like they win! Most importantly, at the end of your term, you must show that you left office with things in better shape than when you arrived. At the end of my term, we improved the school with a gift—we bought a digital billboard for the cafeteria that showed announcements and events. In 2013, when I was selected as a Distinguished Alumnus for the Hall of Honor at Stephen F. Austin High School, that digital billboard was still working to share announcements in the cafeteria!

It was exciting to learn that due to good scores on my PSAT in my junior year, I was named a National Merit Semifinalist. This meant that bundles of school packets began to arrive from all over the country. Each day, the mailbox brought more catalogs and applications from schools that I had not heard of. I was offered trips to visit their campuses and full scholarships for academics!

I got accepted at a few schools, wait-listed at others—and my parents decided that their under-eighteen-year-old was going to attend the University of Texas at Austin *and* would live at home! In my senior year, I started an internship at the Lower Colorado River Authority (LCRA) that would continue through most of college and give me the foundation to build a résumé for future work opportunities. During this job, I learned how to operate office machines, answer the phone, greet executives, and communicate with eye contact and a firm handshake. Working hard at school and having a part-time job was the springboard for many of my career opportunities.

QUESTIONS TO COMB THROUGH

1. Have you ever met a person who needed guidance and, with the help of a few words of wisdom from an elder, changed their path?
2. What was your first leadership role, and what did you learn from it? Did you learn to communicate with people outside your circle of friends? What did you learn from those who are different from you?
3. Who hired you for one of your first jobs? And did you ever reach back to thank them and let them know how your life ended up?

Chapter 5

DEFOLIATION

Cotton plants are defoliated or cleaned of leaves in a process where the leaf detaches and falls off, leaving the cotton boll exposed. This process occurs when plants are mature and removes leaves, stems, and green material (trash) that can stain and contaminate the cotton lint. This allows for better air circulation and reduces toxins, which creates a cleaner, higher-quality yield.

One day, the world of work, school, and life collided in a spectacularly extreme situation!

As a commuter student, I had to park in the farthest lot from my classes on a forty-acre campus. I walked everywhere. While most college students were gaining weight their first year of college, I was losing it with all the walking—which, of course, helped me get modeling assignments. By this time, I was 110 pounds at 5'8", and my new doctor was concerned about my weight, but I ignored the concerns until my menses stopped and lanugo grew. But for modeling, I booked even more work . . .

Debbi received a call for a national model go-see for "brunettes with brown eyes, all-American look" in Dallas. She thought I should go. It would pay thousands of dollars for a national advertising campaign. I agreed and had to ask my UT professors for permission to miss class, my boss at LCRA to miss work, and get an AAA map TripTik to direct me (this is what we used before GPS!) from Austin to Dallas. Dad made sure the Toyota's gas, oil, and tires were ready for the trip. I took off for the casting call with my old Tupperware lunch case and water bottles for the three-hour drive from Austin to Dallas.

A go-see is not guaranteed, and the casting directors would meet hundreds of people. We all knew nothing was promised, but we knew that you just had to be seen, even if a rejection came later. I arrived in Dallas at the go-see and waited until I was called. I walked in, and the casting director simply looked up at me and said, "Why are you here? We are not hiring Black girls." With a wave of her hand, I was dismissed. She did not even take my composite card for future castings. Picking a "look" is normal, but let's face it, *she said the quiet part out loud.*

I understood after four years how the business worked, and even if you are "not the look," most casting directors give you at least a minute. They might say something like, "Thank you for coming," "We will get back to your agent if interested," or simply, "We appreciate your time, and we will hold your card for a future casting." But never had I heard a casting person bring up race.

The call was for brown-eyed brunettes. It would have been so easy for her to have simply remembered to be kind. All she had to do was go through the motions that are part of every go-see: take the comp card, take down my information, snap a few pictures, tell me to walk or pose, and then say what she likely said over a hundred times that day: "We'll get back to your agent. Thank you for coming." That would have allowed me the grace of being able to walk out with my head held high. And a bonus for her, she would have had the file of a person who might be just the person she would need for her next casting call.

After a three-hour drive, waiting, and now facing the drive back, I was absolutely crushed. It was okay not to be booked for a particular assignment, and that is the luck of the draw. Rejection is normalized for all talent based on looks, campaign direction, and more. But blatant racism was still a bit of a shock.

I slunk away, feelings hurt. I called my agent right away. She was livid. She told me to be careful on my drive home and to call her when I arrived at my parents'. The next day, I went back to my internship at LCRA, and my boss, Jerry, and his assistant, Connie, couldn't wait to find out how it went for me. "How'd it go?" they eagerly asked.

I burst into tears.

When I think of that moment, I realize that they must have thought I'd been assaulted or in physical danger. I composed myself and quickly reassured them that nothing untoward had happened, except for meeting a head-on racist who said something that was not needed. Then, through the tears, I told them the story.

They both got angrier and angrier as the story was told.

Jerry said, "I'm going to handle this." He kindly told me to leave his office for a moment. Connie, who was equally infuriated for me, started smiling and said to him, "Oh, I know what you're going to do."

She told me to wait in her office until they called for me. I sat in the leather chair, and a few minutes ticked by. I heard voices on the speakerphone but could not make out the words. I thought they were going to call my agent. I thought they would call the casting company. I began to cry again, thinking as the minutes ticked by, *Oh my goodness, I'm never going to model again.*

Connie came to the door and said, "Come on in." She grabbed a Kleenex for me to wipe my face. I sat in the enormous office, and Jerry was at his desk. Connie sat on the side with her shorthand pad.

Jerry said, "Hillary, I have Robin here." And I heard a Southern voice say, "Hello, Robin. Jerry told me a little bit, but can you tell me what happened yesterday in Dallas?"

I recounted the story and gave her the name of the casting agency and the first name of the person in question. Jerry sat back in his chair with a look that told me it was okay to tell her. When I finished the story, she said, "First of all, Jerry tells me what a good student and intern you have been for the past three years. I happen to be on the board of the company that hosted the go-see and will bring this up at an upcoming meeting. Racist behavior is not okay, and even if you were not right for the part, there is a different way to speak to people. I am sorry that you went through this experience and appreciate your sharing this story. And that casting agency will no longer work for this company. Jerry wouldn't have brought this up to me unless he felt like change needed to happen. I will let him know the outcome and thank you for sharing your story."

And with that, Jerry waved me out of his office, and Connie closed the door.

I didn't know who Hillary was, but I was floored by her confident power. I was at the age when I was still just transitioning as a college student to a young woman working in offices where people can push a button and make something important happen.

I slunk back to my very small office, and got to work—with one thought on my mind: "Am I going to get in trouble?"

About an hour later, he summoned me back to his office. He said, "I want to tell you who that was, and I hope that you know that she was sincere when she spoke to you. That was Hillary Rodham Clinton. She is the wife of the governor of Arkansas named Bill Clinton. I worked with her husband when he ran his first gubernatorial campaign in Arkansas. One day, I think that he will run for president. I will keep you informed, and she said that she wants to write you a letter. And I gave her your address. Was that okay?"

I shook my head yes. And he then said to me, "When other people say things like that, you should understand that they are either trying to hurt your feelings or they are ignorant. I am sorry that her actions affected you, but just know that you will have a bigger future than that casting call."

And with that, I was dismissed to finish my work project. A few weeks later, a letter from Hillary appeared in my mailbox. (I still have it!)

Months later, my agent received a call from that same retailer, specifically requesting me. By then, I was doing runway work for Saks Fifth Avenue and had booked a national ad campaign for Melvin Simon Malls. Even though the company was launching another national campaign, I said, "No, thank you" to them before they had the chance to reject me during another go-see.

In my pride and arrogance, I felt vindicated that they did call for me, but that racist moment was like a bug in a cotton boll—it needed to be combed out before I could go to the next level, and it was important that the experience be processed. Saying no to them was part of the healing process. No one was going to do that to me twice after a six-hour round trip drive to Dallas. No, thank you.

In retrospect, it was my choice not to go, but looking back as an adult: I believe that I should have gone to the second go-see. Even if I had been rejected, it might have opened other doors in a bigger market. I remember that my agent actually double-checked with me: "Are you sure?" She knew that if I were selected, the fee would have paid my rent and tuition for an entire year.

Who knows what opportunity I might have let slip through my fingers by allowing my pride to stand in the way of another bite of the apple? Who knows? I could have been the face of their new campaign. Oh well!

But I learned something quite valuable and gained the awareness that some people really do not care about fairness. Fairness is when someone says, "Hey, you're not the look we want for this campaign. But good luck. So nice to meet you." That's it. All you are guaranteed is an opportunity. It does not mean you will get the spot, but bringing up race in a situation like the casting director did (even though I met all the criteria) is like telling someone that they need to unzip themselves from their skin, and that is just impossible!

Today, I can walk into a room where I am the only Black person, and rather than feel self-conscious, a mind shift takes place, reminding me that they will remember me *because* I am different. It resonates when I think of the many business deals and invitations that have come over the decades. Showing up means doing the work, delivering results, and being there on time, even as you choose to be bold and comfortable in your skin. Most importantly: Do the work!

Living at home while in college, while all my peers were staying in dorms and beginning to have lives of their own, was very challenging. Modeling. Internship job. College. Living at home. I was responsible in all facets, but when I look back, it was not fun. Other kids had a true college experience in dorms, or they went away to college. But I was always working or dealing with a curfew, or my little brother, or frustrated that I had interacted with few new people outside of my in-class friends or high school friends—many of whom had found a new friend circle.

"Look, you are at the University of Texas on a National Merit academic scholarship," my mother had said when I first started college two years earlier. "You are living at home and working at LCRA, and you are modeling too. You can keep saving money, and nothing has to change. Won't that be nice?"

My parents wanted me to be home by 10 PM, and that

was not working for me as a young adult. And as a "townie" going to university down the road, I would continue to sleep in my childhood bed and study behind my childhood bedroom's closed door. Tried to stay focused and tried to ignore the distractions from a smelly teenage brother down the hall. But with few new friends, no dorm experiences, no parties, and only a few group late-night studying sessions in the campus library—it was a cycle of classes, work, home, study, repeat. It did not feel like college!

In high school, I wanted to go away and had used my own money to pay the hefty application fees to Harvard, Princeton, Yale, Stanford, Grinnell, Baylor, Howard, Spelman, and a few others. I did an in-person interview for Princeton and on-campus visits at others including Grinnell. Grinnell accepted me with a full tennis scholarship. UT, Baylor, Howard, and Spelman gave me academic scholarships. But there was the matter of paying out of pocket for living expenses. In order to get federal financial aid or on-campus work study, most families have to fill out FAFSA forms. I had completed the FAFSA forms, stamped them, and given them to my parents to complete so that I could possibly get financial aid from other schools.

Much to my surprise, we never received any offers for financial aid or a confirmation letter. When the aid did not materialize, my mom said it was because she and Dad likely earned too much. When I asked to see the rejection letter, she kept putting me off and would never show me the document. In the end, the only place I could attend without additional financial aid was my hometown school. So I became a Longhorn!

Then came the moment when everything changed, and my helicopter mom crashed.

Today, people call it "adulting." I simply say that this was the night that my mindset changed into an adult's from a childlike dependence. This pivotal moment made me recognize that it was time to grow up, leave the nest, and make my own way.

One afternoon, near the end of my sophomore year, my mother asked, "Robin, will you get the groceries out of the trunk?" So I did.

As I bent down to lift the bags out of the trunk, I noticed something else hidden beneath them. Something flat. Something paper—an envelope. Something familiar. My application for financial aid from two years earlier was still neatly paper-clipped together with the stamped envelopes and the hand-written forms.

She had never completed her section of the forms and certainly never mailed them for evaluation. They had been riding in the trunk with her for over two years! I was livid, came into the house with the bags and the forms, and waved them in front of her. She simply said, "I didn't want to fill them out because I didn't want you to go away . . ." She rattled off countless excuses, but it did not matter.

The simple act of not filling out the forms was the reason that no supplemental financial aid had materialized. She had broken my trust. Even if my parents had made too much money, without the forms, you could not get work study or any school-related support. Where was the supplementation for books or other things with school? If I had not received scholarships, plus worked two jobs (LCRA and modeling), how would school have been paid for?

That night, I was studying for a midterm exam that was 50 percent of my grade, but I could not concentrate. To keep my National Merit scholarship, I still needed to make top grades at UT. There was no time for distractions, but the damage was done. I was very upset.

I realized that my helicopter mother always had to be right . . . her control was at risk if I veered away. So in her effort to exert more control, she pushed me off the cliff!

At some point around seven that night, I took a break from studying and went into the kitchen for a glass of water. My head was full of the words on the pages of the book that I had just walked away from, and I absent-mindedly left the kitchen without turning off the light. As soon as I walked back upstairs to my childhood bedroom and settled back into my desk chair, with my eyes focused on those pages again, I heard rage that I had never heard before.

My mom screamed, "We're trying to save on electricity! If you can't follow my rules, get out of my house!" Those words are all I can remember from the moments that followed.

Since, after all, I was interning at the utility company, I knew that I had used maybe two cents of electricity by leaving the light on. To be honest, I probably said as much in a smart-alecky comment with a disrespectful tone.

That moment marked a major pivot in my life from which there would be no return. It was clear that my mom needed to win. She needed to make me "wrong" to deflect from her actions. She needed to regain her control back from the earlier finding of the FAFSA forms!

A few minutes later, I was suddenly shoved outside, standing on the porch, barefoot, wearing only shorts and a long-sleeve shirt, staring at the front door that had just been slammed in my face. No shoes. No wallet. No keys. We did not have cell phones back then. I was locked out of my childhood home. It would start getting cold as the sun set. All of this happened the night before an exam that determined 50 percent of my grade.

She wants me to grovel and beg to be let inside, I thought. *Well, that's not going to happen.*

But I had midterms the next day. I was supposed to be studying. I was supposed to be focused. A bad grade could put me on academic probation, and I could lose my scholarship. It was near the end of my sophomore year! Halfway through my undergraduate studies. I could not fail. I had to succeed. And I had to get away. It was time to be an adult.

To make matters worse, I had also learned recently that my father had used my identity to get a Sears credit card in my name in 1972, when I was three years old. His name was Rubin, and my name is one vowel away! That was why I could not get credit easily, because I kept having to prove that I had not had a credit card at age three—a card that was not paid on time.

Starting my adult life with bad credit, learning that I had been betrayed, and kicked out of the house on the night before a midterm exam that could impact my scholarship—it was a very upsetting time, but it was also a time to visualize my future, without anyone making a decision for me. Time for adulting!

I started to walk barefoot in my neighborhood toward the elementary school. I knew it had an igloo-style spaceship teetering on a giant spring in the playscape. I climbed inside and curled up. My body heat kept me warm in the small space. It wobbled a bit, and I watched it get dark as people came home. Then I saw lights going out, which is how I deduced it was after the local news. I knew Dad would be home from work around 11 PM. I just had to wait a bit longer.

The chill was horrible. I was shivering. During the silence, I had time to think and consider my options. I gained clarity in that moment of silence with my thoughts. My mother's voice ricocheted in my head—when she said two years earlier, *"Nothing would have to change. Wouldn't that be nice? You can go to the University of Texas and live at home. Won't that be nice?"*

Here I was, a nineteen-year-old young woman still following my mother's instructions and rules from high school—her prerogative, after all, because it was her house. I was missing out on the entire college experience. She forced me to be home by ten at night, even though the library was open all night. I missed new friendships when the campus fun began. And once again, I never went to any parties. Missed the connections people create, which last a lifetime.

Huddled in the spaceship in the school playscape, with my knees up to my chest, it hit me: *I am over age eighteen. A grown woman. It's time for me to have a home of my own. I cannot abide by house rules anymore.*

I said to myself, "It's time to take control of my life. But first I have to take and pass this exam, which is 50 percent of my grade, so I can keep my scholarship." With that thought, the solutions began to present themselves, one at a time, like soldiers reporting for duty:

1. Get an apartment.
2. Ask my LCRA boss, Jerry, and Connie for letters of reference for my new apartment.
3. Get a roommate.
4. Furnish the apartment cheaply. It doesn't have to be fancy; "vintage" will work.
5. Pay for it with my modeling money.

As I stepped out of the spaceship and walked home barefoot, the suburban neighborhood was so quiet that I heard crickets. I had a plan that would move me out of the orbit of my family and eventually, the city, the state, and into a new faraway destination. Never to return except for short visits.

As I walked back to my parents' home barefoot and shivering, I now saw all the lights were burning in the house. Dad's car was in the driveway. My mother opened the door with my first press of the doorbell button. She reached out to hug me, but all I said was, "Don't touch me."

She started to cry and apologize for her actions, but her tears couldn't touch me either. I was done. I could see out of my peripheral vision my father and brother standing there awkwardly. They both looked at my mother and me, back and forth, like they were watching a tennis match.

"You know what you did. You lied about the forms, and now I don't trust you . . . I will be out of your house soon. Please don't bother me now. I have a midterm tomorrow, and I have to pass this exam or I lose my scholarship," I muttered without looking at either of them. "I'm going to study now." With that, I walked up the stairs, entered my room, and closed the door behind me. I was determined to only spend one more night in their house.

In retrospect, much of this was likely rooted in my mother's struggle to stay consistent with her own identity as my protector, even into the years when mothers and daughters naturally gain independence from each other, with the child knowing that they can come home while gently wandering into the world. But it was probably hard for my parents to be empty nesters. She may have wondered: Who was she without protecting her children? Would I adhere to my dietary restrictions? Would I be safe in the big world? She was resisting. My mother was satisfied in knowing we were gathered under her roof at day's end. Dad was on the road, driving a motorcoach on his regular Austin-Houston run. And he just wanted Mom to be happy.

But the boll was bursting, and defoliation was in progress. Like every other family, we rocked from time to time with the usual adolescent angst. We rolled. We pivoted. We talked. We didn't talk. We stayed in our separate rooms behind closed doors. But my brother and I got good grades—mostly A's in our classes. I was on the verge of adulthood—and my parents wanted me to stay in a childhood pattern that needed to change. It was up to me to become an adult!

I got up early the next day. Left the house early to beat traffic, study a bit more, and get a closer parking space. It also meant I left before anyone had the chance to say one word to me. Took the test, which ultimately resulted in a B instead of an A. Left campus with a few apartment rental books and then went to my LCRA internship.

By the time I left work, there were two letters of reference from my job for the apartment manager of the property that was going to meet me in thirty minutes. And with money from modeling jobs, I could pay rent for six months (or more!) in advance.

By chance, earlier that day, I had run into a classmate from Pease Elementary, Stephanie. Our moms had even gone to college together. She and I spoke briefly, and she said that she wanted to move out of the dorm for the next semester. I told her that I was looking for an apartment, and she suggested that we could be roommates! She told me her budget, and that afternoon, I toured and found us a two-bedroom, two-bath apartment on the shuttle bus route to school in the price range we could both afford. It was perched on a hillside with an expansive view. I gave the down payment and moved in the next day with the help of a small moving company and a visit to the discount store for pots and pans and basics. I left a note for my parents and never slept in that home again for more than a short stay.

Stephanie and I lived in that apartment until her graduation, and she went off to dental school.

My brother, Russel, loved that we had an apartment and came over frequently, regularly staying on our sofa. He had known Stephanie since childhood, and he crushed on her and often said he thought she was beautiful. Together we would watch TV, talk about our dreams, and laugh because my brother would tell jokes like Eddie Murphy, who was his comedic model.

My brother and I wanted to start a real estate–related development business of our own. He thought that he would get his engineering degree, and I would take care of the design and finance aspects of the business. "We're a perfect team!" we crowed to each other, marveling at how our skills meshed perfectly to create the ideal package, now that we knew what the business was going to be. And our childhood around our grandfather's properties had taught us about so many things that we were prepared to do together.

But for now, he needed to finish high school and begin his studies at Texas A&M. I needed to keep on studying and start thinking about post-graduation jobs. There would be plenty of time for the future, we promised each other.

My brother was applying to colleges by then, and he only applied to two schools: West Point and Texas A&M, the direct rival to the University of Texas. He got into Texas A&M on a full academic scholarship, and he joined the Corps of Cadets too! He would need the FAFSA forms, too, so that he could have additional financial support for living expenses, but Mom kept saying that we did not qualify. She never showed us proof, just a harumph and a glare that meant "Stop prying." Now it made sense—she had never even followed through on my forms, and she wasn't going to do it for him either.

Ultimately, it forced my brother to get a job in addition to his Corps of Cadets duties, and it was overwhelming—working at an off-campus night shift job since he could not get an on-campus role without the FAFSA forms. So he made a fateful choice about school, and we would find out soon enough that Russel was carrying a secret.

QUESTIONS TO COMB THROUGH

1. Have you ever experienced something you thought was the end of something, but with a mindset shift, you realized was really a beginning?
2. Have you ever learned something that caused a profound shift in you and how you viewed another person?
3. At what age did you "adult," and do you feel like you are using your generational wealth of information to guide you toward your dreams?

Chapter 6

HARVEST

Determining the optimal time of harvest is based on when the bolls are open and dry. Recognizing that moment requires experience and careful observation. The first defoliation removes leaves to create a cleaner harvest and provides clear visuals of how the harvest is progressing. Then, you need to determine if any remaining weeds and debris need to be removed to ensure an unobstructed path.

I was nineteen. "Charles" was twice my age. He would ask me, "What is your dream? What is your goal? Do you want to stay in Austin? Why don't you spend the summer in California?" I had just ended a college romance and met this Dallas native who was a consultant at LCRA. For my 21st birthday, he invited me to dinner to celebrate, during which he spoke about why he'd left Texas. Charles told me about how he left Texas after graduating from college, moved to the West Coast to work in a global firm, and how he had traveled the world.

Meeting someone who was a world-traveler from Texas made me realize that my thoughts about transitioning away from home were okay. His understanding of my big-dream reality was refreshing, because I felt that Austin, Texas, in that era, was limiting for a person of color. Today, both the city and the state have progressed, but in the late 1980s, there were still significant career mindset barriers for both women and diverse people.

Charles sat with me one day to help me write a real résumé that highlighted the skills I had developed at LCRA. During the process, he peppered me with questions about my vision for my future. I sat still in the conference room and responded, "I want to be involved in real estate in some way, but I also want to be on TV and sell stuff in stores. I want to have a brand like Martha Stewart."

He looked at me and said, "You can do that, but you need to see more of the world, so you have perspective."

With that, I cheekily asked him the same thing: "What is your dream?" He responded, "I hope to get married one day, and to travel globally, and to spend time with my niece, brother, and sister-in-law. I have professional success, but it is time to focus on my personal life."

His nuanced answer to that question has stayed with me. There is a point in everyone's life when you have success in one area, and you may want to expand your efforts in another. It is good to have a plan.

We had become close while working together on this consulting assignment focused on demand-side management (DSM) tools that LCRA could implement for efficiency and residential cycling technologies. My role was to gather quantitative data for his team to analyze and evaluate, and then sum up data points in a qualitative report for leadership.

During his time in Austin, he became a "life" guide for me, and I became a "style" guide for him, to ensure he did not get a tourist version of Austin. He had a nice long-term hotel space and a standard auto rental, until I told him that he could get a better vehicle for the same price from a certain rental firm. He changed to a sportier car and upgraded from a hotel room to an actual townhouse for less money. And then we started our foodie and cultural excursions.

He took me to dinners at places like Jean Pierre's Upstairs and Jeffrey's, and I took him to places like Kerbey Lane Cafe, Chuy's, Cisco's, Hyde Park Bar & Grille, Matt's El Rancho, and The County Line. Plus, he attended a few fashion shows. We heard music at venues including Antone's, Austin City Limits, Cactus Café, Stubb's, and Liberty Lunch. The early iteration of South by Southwest was evolving from the original Austin Aqua Fest, so there was a lot of media, music, fashion, and buzz about Austin.

On October 17, 1989, the San Francisco earthquake occurred, and Charles flew back to see if his home in the Marina District had survived. When he returned, he talked about the pancaked homes in the Marina District and said that he was lucky, but many of his neighbors were not. We went to dinner, and he shared that he had met with his team. They wanted to invite me to apply for a paid internship for eight weeks in the summer of 1990.

"Yes!" I shrieked. And then he reminded me that I was only applying and would be competing against several others. He told me to never again say yes to a job until I fully understood the requirements, expectations, and salary—and to always be ready to negotiate. After another review, I submitted my newly formatted résumé and waited eagerly for a response.

In January, the letter arrived. I brought it into the office and read it aloud to Charles, Jerry, and Connie. "Congratulations, you have been accepted into the summer 1990 internship class at XYZ firm located in Oakland, CA—just a short train ride from San Francisco. Please contact our team to discuss start date, compensation, and short-term rentals."

Everyone congratulated me, but they already knew because Charles had informed them. Much to my surprise, the entire office came down the hall and clapped, a tower of cupcakes arrived, and there was a gift: my first set of grown-up luggage!

About two months before my trip, I was hospitalized again for a reaction to something, and I was determined to get better in time for the internship. The doctor gave me an IV treatment that cleared all the bacteria, good and bad. I was weak and lost about ten pounds from my already thin frame. Anything I ate made me feel awful. The doctor said that he was worried about the growth of lanugo, a sign of anorexia, on my body.

He told me that I had to eat, as he was very concerned.

I did not tell my parents since I was an adult, and the doctor could not tell them either and could only make suggestions that whatever I ate should be healthy. I was determined that nothing would stand in the way of this trip to San Francisco. Plus, I was getting booked for more modeling jobs due to my waiflike appearance—I think I weighed 112 pounds—and got booked for a Chanel runway show, which was so dreamy. Through that one runway show booking, I earned more than enough to pay for my summer sublet and my share of the rent for the summer in the Austin apartment, even though I would be away.

Summer 1990 was a few weeks away, and I was overjoyed—San Francisco! This was before Airbnb, so a short-term rental meant perusing want ads, calling colleges, and asking friends to send you the local newspaper if you could not access a copy in the school library using LexisNexis.

I found a summer sublet, and a UT friend from Italy named Marco agreed to pick me up from the airport in his vintage convertible. He had just graduated and been accepted to a Stanford graduate program.

The pending visits by both Nelson Mandela and Mikhail Gorbachev, who would be in the Bay Area that summer, made the experience beyond exciting. It was thrilling to have opportunities to see or hear global figures and spend my first length of time away from Texas. There was so much to see and experience over eight weeks. I created a grid for myself with three columns—must, maybe, and miscellaneous—to outline all the things to do over the summer!

Growing up in Texas, the heat begins to permeate the earth around April and reaches a peak in August and early September. The weather in Texas (and other parts of the South) creates perfect conditions for growing cotton. Planting begins in the spring, and harvest occurs in the latter part of summer and early fall. When the cotton is harvested, the gin process begins—opening the boll to get the debris out, removing stems, and then combing the cotton.

The summer of 1990 was like harvest time: traveling to another part of the country, chasing a dream, and making adult choices on my own. My family had poured so much into me, ingredients that would propel me forward, and now it was a chance to examine myself: What was my ethical and moral compass, my work ethic? What debris did I have, or what would be revealed during this summer?

My sublet at the Nob Hill Chateau was on the corner of Pine and Powell, a 250-square-foot studio with a Murphy bed, chair, and bay window on the sunny side of the street, offering a view of the cable cars along with the grinding sounds and regular cadence of the clanging bell. There was no television, so my list of to-dos was being checked off quickly. All I did was explore the city unless there was rain. On those days, I had magazines and books to read since this was before smartphones. And it was fun to sit in that sunny bay window to watch the tourists hanging out of the cable cars while taking photos with their disposable cameras. Since I did not consider myself a tourist, given my residency, it was fun to take pictures of them!

Recalling the *Mister Rogers' Neighborhood* TV show or the Rice-a-Roni commercials, it was always a joy to see the trolleys and hear the clanging bells, leading me to pinch myself, and marvel, *Am I really here?* There were a few times when I just rode the cable cars from end to end to learn the city layout and found it was more affordable than a taxi.

I only had $1,200 budgeted in cash to carry me over until my first paycheck two weeks later. I discovered that Chinatown was just around the corner from Nob Hill, and I learned how to use chopsticks that summer. Most of the dishes did not have preservatives, as they were freshly made, so the food did not make my throat close up. Fresh vegetables, brown rice, lots of fresh air, no pollen, and walking were just the prescription I needed to renew. Since it was so chilly, walking or hill climbing did not result in the ubiquitous sweat stains that one would see during a Texas summer. I was still unable to eat much, and the clothing I had bought for the internship hung on me loosely.

I learned about the 1906 fire in San Francisco that required the city to rebuild itself. I watched the aftermath of the AIDS epidemic as entire blocks were affected, and I learned about the Haight-Ashbury area where people were "tuning out" to music from Janis Joplin (a fellow Texan!), plus the tech community focused on new internet technology—in retrospect, I wish that I had invested back then!

And the architecture: bay windows and pocket doors have become part of my signature design work, along with the power of natural light through uncovered windows. I kept my windows open just a little bit to let the sea breeze into my studio. The difference between natural air and air conditioning changed my breath. I began to have less labored wheezing and almost no sneezing. My inflammation and reactions to pollen lessened. I felt healthier and did not have to use my asthma inhaler very often.

Treks to Carmel, Berkeley, Palo Alto, Los Angeles, and Napa created some memorable moments, in addition to the traditional tourist moments like Ghirardelli Square, Lombard Street, Coit Tower, and Alcatraz. But what really captured me was listening to music and seeing performances. One show produced by SFJAZZ was called the Jazz Tap Summit, where I saw Honi Coles, the Nicholas Brothers, Bunny Briggs, and Savion Glover!

Every day felt like an adventure as I walked out of my studio, and the only decision to make was: right, left, BART, or cable car! Freedom!

The wildest thing was the reverse commute on the BART subway train: going from chilly San Francisco to summer temperatures in Oakland. It was always at least fifteen degrees warmer. The office was located in the Citibank (now Citigroup Center) building on the shore of Lake Merritt, where people would be wearing short sleeves, and I would be taking off my coat. Two seasons in fifteen minutes!

Charles had some friends who lived near the Stanford campus in Palo Alto, and we visited them and felt the temperature warming up even more. On one visit, our host was making lemonade, and she asked me to get her some lemons. I stepped toward the refrigerator, but instead, she directed me to the backyard so that I could pluck them right off the tree!

Other friends from the office invited me to the Concours

d'Elegance in Pebble Beach, and we all drove up together. One of the interns had family who lived in Carmel, so I saw immense wealth for the first time.

What lessons was I learning during this trip? I was learning about work, independence, and building a résumé and connections. Plus, with new friends, I was learning the unspoken rules about dress, language, and manners around immense wealth and privilege, which demand relaxing and operating at a slower pace, like lingering conversations over lunch—not just eating.

When driving outside of the cities, we would see migrants in fields picking strawberries (Santa Cruz), garlic (Gilroy), and grapes (Napa)—so evocative of the sharecroppers and migrants in Texas. I realized that any mention of my background could ostracize me from the new crowd that I was being accepted into—and I wrote about my thoughts in a diary.

Summer was speeding by, and I realized that I was now living in two worlds. Life was opening itself up to me like a cotton boll, but I was also seeing the debris inside through a different lens. It was harvesting time.

Remember that my father's older brothers went to military service, sending part of their pay home so that my grandparents could buy a house and Dad and his next older brother and sister could focus on school instead of cotton fields. Had it not been for their sacrifices, my dad might not have graduated from high school, might never have met my mother—and their lives might have been different.

Uncle John was one of those brothers whom I remembered

meeting as a child when he and his whole family drove to Texas in 1977 when Grandpapa passed away. They stayed for a month with my aunts, uncles, and grandparents. All of them had California style with afros, cargo pants, tank tops, and a different way of speaking. We went roller skating at the local rink, and they could skate backward and do cool moves to the disco music.

My brother and I had never skated and could barely stand up, but the blisters on our feet were worth it. We were hanging out with our cool California cousins. They were all at least ten years older, but it was so much fun! Because of my sepia-toned memories, I wanted to reconnect with them again since they all lived in Oakland.

Before returning home to Austin, I realized that each call home to request my Uncle John's phone number or address in Oakland was rebuffed by my parents, who kept saying they would get the information to me. I finally called my aunt, and she gave me the information with a cautionary warning to understand that several of his children were in the throes of addiction. I didn't understand their subtle warnings, but I would soon learn what the harvest had sown from that side of the family.

"Oh no," my parents were quick to respond when I said that I was going to visit Uncle John. "You should only visit with him, not go to the house. I don't think that you understand what is happening to your cousins. The situation is different, and you don't need to go visit them. He'll understand that you are really busy. One day, we will go out together to see them."

I said, "But I just want to say hi, and my office is in Oakland," I reassured them. "I haven't been to that part of Oakland, but don't forget I work in the town every day. I will get a rental car for this one trip. It'll be fine."

Only ten miles away. I was in town. I was *there*! Why not?

My parents were direct. My aunt was direct. Maybe I did not hear the nuance in their pushback. I thought they were just worried about me driving and getting lost, so I called my Uncle John and suggested we meet in San Francisco or near Lake Merritt.

"Oh, that won't work for me," Uncle John said over the phone. "I don't have a working car right now."

That puzzled me. So, I tried a few other scenarios involving him and his family coming into San Francisco. He dodged each one with one excuse after another.

"Okay, fine," I said. "I'll come see you."

"Oh no," he quickly answered. "You really don't have to."

"Of course I do," I insisted. "We're family. It will be great to see my cousins again."

He paused and didn't say anything for a moment as though he knew my determination would overcome any objections. "Well, come early in the day if you're coming, and I want you on the road before it is dark," he firmly instructed. "No later. And make sure to call me first."

When Charles caught wind of my plans, he also tried to stop me. He asked, "What's the address?" I told him. "Do you realize that's in the zone where even the police won't go unless it's an emergency call? Your parents were right. You should skip this idea. Everyone will understand. But if you really go, then get out of there before dark."

But he could tell by the look in my eye that I was determined. This was before mobile phones, so there was no way to communicate without calling someone on a landline.

Of course, I had heard news reports about the crack epidemic that had the entire country by the throat at that time. I read the newspapers. In Austin, I had seen the gaunt figures on East 11th Street. But those headlines were about *other* people, *other* families, *other* neighborhoods, and I assumed it did not have anything to do with me or my family.

I picked up my rental car and set up my custom AAA TripTik on the passenger side so I could refer to the driving directions. I tried to call before I left, but the phone sounded a beep-beep-beep, followed by an announcement that the phone was disconnected.

Crossing the Oakland Bay Bridge was not as spectacular as the Golden Gate Bridge, but as I drove farther into Oakland, the reality set in. When I exited the freeway, there was a sign stating, "No police patrols in this area after dark unless an emergency." The area looked increasingly blighted.

I followed the directions and made a right turn onto their street. I had dressed up in a navy pleated skirt, white silk top, bolero-style checkered jacket, and carried a Coach handbag. My rental car was a Ford Taurus. In retrospect, I probably looked like a government official or caseworker.

When I turned onto their street, kids were playing outside everywhere, adults were on their porches, and teens were leaning up against cars. *A good sign*, I thought. And then suddenly, everyone disappeared. The street was clear. It was like the apocalypse. All of a sudden, no one was outside. You could hear crickets chirp, if there were any.

When I knocked, no one came to the door. But then I heard a movement, at child level, and I knocked again, and said loudly through the burglar bars, "Hi, I'm your cousin Robin from Texas." I guess everyone could hear me, because the door opened and Uncle John and a small child stood there smiling. Then, neighbors peeked out their windows, and some came out of their houses. People were curious to meet Uncle John's niece, and he waved over some boys and told them to watch my car.

I entered the dark house as the electricity was not on. He opened the curtains to let some light in through the windows, and I saw some teens surrounding my rental car. The house had a strange smell to it, and he left the front door open for fresh air. The furniture had seen better days. I was polite and well-mannered, and he commented on how put-together I looked.

From the back of the house, one of the cousins I remembered from roller skating came out to say hello. He looked different—this flashy dresser who had taught me how to roller skate did not look like the person I remembered. He said, "Hey, you want some BBQ—we don't have a lot in the house for a guest. Give me $40, and I will go get some." In the corner of my eye, I saw my uncle shaking his head.

"Okay, great idea," I said. I reached into my pocketbook and gave him $50, as I still did not understand the situation.

"The barbecue place is closed right now," my uncle said resignedly. "In fact, it's been closed all day today."

My cousin flashed a smile. I never saw him again, and that BBQ never arrived.

I stayed for less than an hour, and my uncle sounded weary. It was obvious that his health was failing. He spoke of his fear of going to the VA hospital because he did not trust his home would be managed while away, and he had to take care of this little child, who I learned was around ten years old.

A weird smell permeated the room. I glanced into the kitchen and could spot the skittering of bugs on the piles of dirty dishes. I was saddened, but still, we politely made some stiff small talk for a little while.

Uncle John asked, "How's your daddy? And your mama? How's your little brother? What brings you to Oakland? How much longer will you be here? You look so professional. All grown up. You're so beautiful. Your daddy told us you're modeling now. Stand up and do a little spin."

"Fine. He says to say hello. She's fine too," I replied.

I stood and gave a twirl with my pleated skirt flaring out. Then a little voice piped up out of the gloom, with a question I hadn't prepared for. "Are you a princess? Can I sit on your lap?"

"What's your name?" I asked.

She shyly responded. "I want to be pretty and nice like you when I grow up. And you smell good."

With this child on my lap, it was obvious that the situation was fraught and almost all my uncle's children had fallen to the temptations of crack. My $50 was likely contributing to further addiction. It was time to go, almost dark. No need to wait any longer for the BBQ. In hindsight, it would have been better to have given my uncle the $50 bill or helped him turn his electricity back on.

And here I was, all dressed up, heading back to Nob Hill for another week—and then back home to Austin. I was honored to see him and yet saddened to be there. It was the last time I would be in his presence before he passed.

I politely made my way through the gaggle of neighbors who crowded my uncle's front yard. They peppered me with surface questions: "You are so pretty, and Mr. John told us that you are a model. What about my daughter—do you think she could model?" "Do they ride horses in Texas? Are you coming back? We should have a cookout next time, right, John?"

I realized that these folks were hospitable even with little means. When I glanced in my rearview mirror, the street waved goodbye, and I could see my uncle thanking the boys for watching my car. That's what good neighbors do for each other.

I realized at that moment that my future had been built on the back of this man and my dad's older brothers. He was not given the opportunities that my dad had, and his service in the military did not have the desired result, with limited access to the GI Bill. There was no one to reach back to provide a path for him.

Through the hard work of my elder uncles, my dad got the benefit of moving to Austin, graduating from high school, and meeting my mom, which let them create a middle-class life for me. And here I was in the home of a man who had worked hard all his life, and he was likely worse off. He had been a soldier sending his paychecks home, and now he was in a redlined neighborhood, in a home that did not even have electricity.

This hero in my father's life story was living a blighted life.

As I entered the freeway back to my studio in Nob Hill, the primary thought at the top of my mind choked me up: *What if my life had been my cousin's life?* I realized that while my parents and aunt had tried to warn me, it had been good for me to see things for myself.

As the years passed, I always wondered what happened to that little girl. My aunt kept up with her and shared that my Uncle John fiercely protected her, walking her to school each day, and locking his bedroom door so she could stay on a cot in his room and not witness the situation related to the other family members.

And when Uncle John passed away, she enlisted in the military and never stopped telling people that she wanted to be like the princess she met, who was her cousin.

When I reconnected with and spoke to the now–young lady in 2020, I learned that she had grown up to be a lawyer and served in the military on the JAG team. We're still in touch, even to this day, and she remembers the impact my short visit had on her life. She stayed focused and was able to escape her narrow world—she persevered and stayed focused on her dreams.

QUESTIONS TO COMB THROUGH

1. What internship did you have in college that changed your life?
2. When was the first time that you straddled two worlds: your hometown and the future?
3. When you visit with certain relatives, do you realize how your life journey is different from their path? Have you ever influenced a relative to chase their dream?

Part 2

Ambitious Journey

Chapter 7

READY TO MOVE

Cotton is made ready for moving in a process called module building. Harvested cotton is collected from the field and compressed into large rectangles called bales, which makes the cotton ready to transport to the cotton gin.

When I returned from my summer in San Francisco, my outlook was different. The past was the prologue to my future—the "why" questions were answered at the same time that the Y in the road was paving itself. I had inhabited the world that was my future—global, corporate, cultured. The bookend of that experience was the visit to my uncle's home, a recognition of the past.

Based on my experience, it is my recommendation that parents allow their children to go away to college, so they may wish to return home. In my case, my escape was leaving my hometown after graduating. (Let me interject by saying that it was wonderful to grow up in Austin, and I love being a Texan, but it was time to explore the world!) That summer internship in California made me ready to move out. It had become clear that my dreams were too big for my hometown.

Remember that I did not go away to college, so leaving for eight weeks led to a big stretch in my growth. Upon my return, there was both discomfort and a little nostalgia. What was certain was that some things that were previously normal were now things that were irritating: the August heat, the burning of my legs when getting into a hot car, the insects, the pollen. And the criticism.

"You are different," was an observation made by my roommate, brother, parents, and friends. I guess that was true. But the lesson learned was the truth: that they had stayed the same, while I had grown.

The old me was a suit that would not fit anymore. Certain things were different—I was eating less red meat and more vegetables. I was exercising more and eating healthier instead of starving myself to stay thin. I was proficient in using chopsticks and had less interest in local gossip. Or was it a new sense of comfort in affluent settings and sitting differently? Less perfect posture, and more calmness in gesture and poise. These were all small things, but they were visible to those who had remained the same and noticed different energy and mannerisms.

At the time, hearing this commentary felt like criticism. Looking back, they were likely feeling that my energy was different, but they did not have the words. To me, it felt hurtful, as though they did not approve of the new me, even though I was fulfilling all the goals and expectations laid out for me: to be independent, excel, and use my education.

Unfortunately, growing up with orthopedic shoes, braces, asthma, and allergies, speaking properly, and being different made me susceptible to hearing general comments as criticism. To this day, I wrestle with that tendency as I am very spongy, absorbing the emotions of others.

Remember always that to become your best self . . . you must comb out the debris. Your reality will come to fruition when you create a vision board for your life, so you actually have a plan and know where you want to go. I had a plan now. Where was I going? I was moving away from my hometown and toward a career, not just a job.

Prior to that summer, I had no plan. I simply wanted a job and assumed I would move into a full-time role at LCRA after my paid internship. But going away made me take the on-campus job fairs seriously. By this time, even though Jerry had now moved to Washington, DC, to work on the ENERGY STAR program, and a new executive had moved into his office, my first day back at LCRA for my fourth year as an intern was a wake-up call.

Connie exclaimed, "Oh my goodness. Girl, look at you. So grown up. You look so polished." She was so proud. She now reported to the executive in Jerry's old office. My cubicle was still the same; in fact, everything looked the same. But everything inside me had changed in only eight weeks.

Soon, I would move on too. I was encouraged to look further than LCRA and my hometown for job opportunities. My senior year at UT meant having a wider vision for jobs and a realization that I could live anywhere. There were no limits in thinking about my future, as there might have been in the past.

So I picked up the *Daily Texan* school newspaper and signed up for the job fair interviews at the Career Services office. I showed up to the fall college fairs with a lot of energy, wearing my navy-blue skirt suit and carrying résumés printed on vellum cotton paper. I applied for jobs on both coasts and in London after listening to recruiters from different industries who shared big visions and global office locations. This career fair process was both daunting and eye-opening, as I realized all the competition in the room were also looking for jobs. But I had an advantage: work experience on my résumé!

What did I know? I knew my first real job would not be in Austin. I was a townie, having attended schools in Austin, graduated from Austin High, and would soon matriculate from UT. Everything was possible, and I was ready to move—and my hometown was not my destination. Simple thought: the cotton plant in the field will not look like its final destination as a fabric.

One evening after my return, my parents asked, "Why would you spend $80 to go to a Sade concert? You have her records; you can hear her on the radio for free. And she's on MTV too. Why would you spend that kind of money?"

I responded, "Because I want to experience her performance and support the artist. I have never been to a real concert at the

Erwin Center, except for school events. So my friends and I are going to go hear her sing and then have dinner at Hyde Park Grille."

They both shook their heads. Their next sentence might have been, "And there is good food here at home, so why do you need to go eat out too?" but I just glared at them, so they held their tongues. We were trying to find a common ground now that they were getting used to being empty nesters.

My parents later told me that they felt like their daughter left for San Francisco, and now a new young adult person inhabited her skin. Changes that might have happened if I were away at college were happening before their eyes, and it was too much, too fast for them.

Now, my wardrobe was West Coast business casual, not jeans and a shirt. I walked differently because my core was stronger due to treks up and down the hills in San Francisco. My shoulders were less constricted because I had spent two months learning how to breathe fully without my throat closing up.

Even my doctor described my body as less inflamed, because my lungs and gut had been able to heal. I was much thinner but was healthier. The new me felt and looked better.

That fall, I traveled alone to Washington, DC, for a weekend visit to the museums and to an interview. I decided to visit Congressman J. J. Pickle, whose granddaughter was a classmate of mine in high school. When I entered the congressional office building, I entered his office and asked to say hello. The intern at the desk said, "I'm sorry. You are not on his schedule. Would you like to leave a note? How may I help you?"

I told him that I was just going to say hello and said my name. The intern glared at me for a moment, and then he got up and walked back to the inner office. Within seconds, he exited the congressman's office and looked bewildered as Congressman Pickle came out and gave me a big hug and invited me into his office. I stuck my tongue out at the intern and flounced into the inner office.

Congressman Pickle asked about my parents and what I was planning to do after college. (My father had driven many bus charters for LBJ, the congressman, and other dignitaries.) He then asked if I wanted a private tour of the Capitol. I said yes, and he said that the intern would take me around. Our meeting lasted probably ten minutes, and when he walked me back to the front desk, he said to the intern, "Take Robin over to the Capitol on the train. And accompany her for whatever she wants to do . . ." Looking back, I do not remember what I wanted to do, but he was my guide for the next few hours. A meet-cute for my next boyfriend.

During our walk, I learned that he was from a prominent Black family in Austin, and he was a Harvard student. His family knew some of my high school friends. A few days later, my phone rang, and he asked me out on a date when he got back home for the holidays. He said that he had spent several days trying to find out how to get in touch. It was nice to be pursued. I agreed to that date, and we spoke almost every day by phone until that Thanksgiving. He had big goals, and we became inseparable.

In hindsight, this began a terrible pattern of following a guy for love instead of carrying on with my own path. Instead of the West Coast, I started looking at jobs on the East Coast—Boston specifically. I finished classes in December 1991 and was hired to start work at a Boston consulting firm with my start date in January 1992—without any break between studies and working. I was exhausted but exhilarated, and the adrenaline carried me through.

My brother was now a student at Texas A&M, and one day, before I left for Boston, he called and asked me to meet him at our parents' house because he had to tell everyone something—a secret. I arrived at the appointed time and saw my brother's red motorcycle parked on the porch.

We all saw that he looked serious and had some papers in an envelope on the table.

"I am going to do my patriotic duty to join the Army for Operation Desert Storm. I am joining several corps members and will be taking a sabbatical from Texas A&M. I have already enlisted and ship out in a few days for Basic Training. I need to list my beneficiaries and need some information so I can add it to the forms. I hope you will make it to the Basic Training graduation ceremony," said my brother.

I gasped. My mom clutched Dad's hands. My dad just stood up, shook his hand, and calmly asked, "Are you sure?" Then, he hugged him.

I sat at the dining room table with tears in my eyes, stunned and in absolute disbelief that my brother would leave Texas A&M in his sophomore year, put his full engineering scholarship on hold, and quit the Corps of Cadets. My mom just sat there stunned, with her hands clasped in prayer.

I gasped again. Like I could not breathe. I had a foreboding that he would never come home, like he was going to die. I could not shake the feelings and started to cry. My feelings did not matter. He was already enlisted. He was moving on—in his way.

He left for Basic Training and was stationed in several places but spent the longest time on the DMZ in Korea. He began training to become an Army Ranger while serving in the PsyOps division.

Weeks earlier, I had read aloud to my parents, "Congratulations, you have been hired for an analyst role at Temple, Barker & Sloane (later acquired by Mercer Management Consulting and today known as Oliver Wyman) in our Lexington, Massachusetts office for a base salary, plus a signing bonus." I beamed. My parents looked at each other.

Dad had an expression on his face that I could not read. Mom looked upset, and in an agitated tone, said, "You did not ask my permission to apply for jobs outside of Texas. I had a job lined up for you at a state agency. I don't want you to take that job so far away."

"I already accepted. And I am going," I replied. As a twenty-one-year-old, this was not the reaction I expected. Other offers had come in from Houston, Dallas, and West Coast firms.

My mom stormed away, went upstairs, and slammed the bedroom door. Dad just stood there and asked to see the letter. He read it and said softly, "Congratulations. Your mom is just upset because she wants to keep you close. Your brother is gone, and it is a lot for her. But that is a lot of money they are offering to pay you. Do your best, and I am going up to check on your mother."

And with that, the room was empty.

I thought to myself, *They have done everything to make me believe that I am worthy, and now that an opportunity presents itself, I am made to feel bad. At least I am trying to be independent and become an adult.*

A few weeks later, a haphazard graduation event was organized by my mother with some relatives. It did not go well, because she did not tell me in advance. Since she had given me the cold shoulder since my announcement, I had made plans with other people to celebrate. I only saw my grandparents and a few others for a moment, but it was a clear message that my big day and future were not celebrated, and it hurt my feelings.

I bought a new, reliable Honda Accord, and within three weeks, I left Texas.

On the day I left, my dad stood outside to wave goodbye. My mom barely hugged me and did not even come outside. So as I backed out of the driveway, I resolved to never come back home, as it did not feel like I was welcome, and I did not live there anymore.

I stopped by my boyfriend's (the congressional intern) house to pick him up, and his parents loaded us up with snacks for the long drive to Boston. They sent us off with hugs and waves. Such different energy . . . pride and excitement compared to the somber mood at my parents' home.

Along the way in Kentucky, we were keeping up with traffic, but we were pulled over by an unmarked patrol car. My boyfriend seethed in the passenger seat, saying under his breath, "It is because we are driving while Black (DWB) in a new car with paper tags."

But my mindset was different. I did not think like him. I knew that we were speeding, but I was keeping up with traffic in the far-left lane. My thought process was that he just picked us out by chance. There were several reasons for my optimism—my mom was employed by the Texas Department of Public Safety (a.k.a. the Texas Rangers), and I knew the protocol: Answer the questions politely and follow instructions without abrupt movements. *All officers just want to get home to their families at night.* I was not scared or upset. Clueless, maybe, but not worried or upset. It would just be a speeding ticket.

The officer approached the car after I pulled over to the far-right shoulder.

"Hello, Officer," I said in a happy voice while leaving my hands on the wheel.

"Do you know how fast you were going? License and registration? Where are you headed? Do you have any dead bodies in the trunk?"

I laughed and said, "No, sir, I was speeding, and I was just keeping up with traffic, and no, we don't have any dead bodies in the trunk." I reached over to get my registration and opened my handbag for my license. "We are headed to Boston. He goes to Harvard, and I just got my first job after graduating from the University of Texas!"

The officer was in plainclothes with a badge on his belt and in an unmarked car. His eyebrows raised when I said Harvard. He asked to see my boyfriend's student ID. When he saw that, I guess he realized that if he had pulled us over for nefarious reasons, it would end up in the headlines. Or maybe he was just charmed by my happy-go-lucky demeanor—no hostility, just openness.

Within minutes, without even calling it in, he just said,

"Slow down and drive safe. And keep your valuables hidden, like that Apple computer box. Put a blanket over it." He handed back our documents and let us go.

QUESTIONS TO COMB THROUGH

1. Are you susceptible to hearing comments as criticism?
2. What was the meet-cute for your first romantic partner in college? What happened to that relationship?
3. Have you ever been uncomfortable with someone's change to their trajectory? Do you celebrate their decisions as they might celebrate yours?

[illegible]

QUESTIONS TO COME THROUGH

[illegible]

Chapter 8

Show Me the Money

After being graded, ginned, and baled, cotton is sold through various channels, including direct sales, brokers, cooperatives, and major exchanges. As a commodity, the price is based on many factors, such as quality and market demand.

Upon arrival in Boston, I met the right people through the proper Southern introductions. The mother of a high school friend knew someone in Boston, who made proper introductions to a certain social circle. My first calling card was with Nina Doggett, a very elegant lady who invited me to lunch at her women's club. The all-Black waitstaff gawked when I arrived and held me at the front door to verify that I was truly a guest of someone. They were peeking through the kitchen window, likely wondering *Who is she?*, as I saw no other people of color in the dining room except the staff. Nina did not notice the gawking, as only someone who has a distinguished social standing would feel comfortable inviting me into that room.

I remember wearing a salmon-pink suit, like Elle in *Legally Blonde*. Everyone else had muted shades of white, beige, navy, or black. I stood out like an Easter egg. Thankfully, at that first meeting, she knew that I did not know anything about Boston or have any airs. I was just being myself. And I think she complimented me on the color, but I quickly realized that muted shades were probably better in the Northeast.

Nina was so kind and has remained a mentor. She quickly taught me the social norms and unspoken rules about New England. Often the first questions are "Where do you summer?" and "What school did you attend?" She said that I should reply with kindness, and if I did not feel like answering, to simply say that I had recently moved to Boston from Texas, and then the questions might be different.

Nina suggested that I join the Boston Symphony Orchestra's (BSO) Board of Overseers since I enjoyed classical music. With her recommendation, I became one of the youngest members of the board, giving me the opportunity to meet Seiji Ozawa, Yo-Yo Ma, Ann Hobson Pilot, and John Williams (and watched him pass the Boston Pops baton to Keith Lockhart), and attend Tanglewood to see performances by James Taylor and other musicians.

Within months, I was invited to reinvigorate the BSO Crescendo Concert Access Initiative focused on young professionals from twenty to forty. The strategy was to set aside a limited block of tickets so that young people could attend concerts to support the arts, gain access to culture, and allow them to meet a group of like-minded young professionals. Crescendo worked like a charm and dropped the average age of BSO attendees from sixty-five to forty-two. Membership in Crescendo gave young professionals access to four concerts and up-close interactions with the conductor or a featured musician. The first event sold out within four weeks and solidified the excitement of involving musicians who could educate the youthful audience. Attendees bought a subscription of tickets for two orchestral concerts and two Pops concerts.

At our first event, Seiji Ozawa appeared. Later, Keith Lockhart, the most eligible bachelor and the new Boston Pops conductor, told the group, “When the drums sound, that means the horses are galloping.” He further explained the music so that by intermission, everyone felt like they understood what they were listening to. It also helped when word got out and the newspaper wrote a story about Crescendo—with the full support of the BSO behind this initiative to expand the arts and philanthropy of young professionals.

I was also introduced to Bennie and her husband, Fletcher “Flash” Wiley, through my Texas friends. Bennie is one of the most amazing people I have ever met. She created and led The Partnership organization, and both she and her husband were so kind to me. I was one of the younger Fellows in the organization, which brought together diverse business leaders in Boston to build a global community with insight into local and global affairs. Having familiarity with many of the names and faces in the group because of pages in magazines and the news was very different now that I was in the room speaking to them directly. It was a milestone moment to begin to understand how far my life had changed from my hometown.

Initially, I was learning how to be an outsider navigating an elite world—until ultimately, I realized that I had been welcomed with a seat at the table. And it was time to get comfortable with this amazing group of people who led business, cultural, and social circles.

Even today, I remain in touch with Nina Doggett and Bennie Wiley. Both women showed me leadership, empathy, and wisdom during the most challenging moment of my life. In April 1993, less than two years after arriving in Boston, my brother died while on a brief leave from his station-post at the DMZ. I was bereft as I learned the meaning of a Gold Star family.

Two months earlier. My brother and I had stayed in constant touch with letters and a few overseas phone calls. In many of his letters, we talked about what type of entrepreneurial business we would form together after his stint of duty was over. He mentioned modular building technology, which he had learned about, and it melded his love of technology with my love for real estate. With his engineering background and my business experience, we thought we would create a development firm.

One morning, I was awakened by my new mobile phone. I screamed. I had spent the night in my boyfriend's dorm at Harvard, and my phone rang multiple times. It was my landlord from my small rental house in Somerville, where I rented the top floor. He informed me that my brother was there, and he was napping in my apartment. My brother had a brief leave from Fort Bragg, and he had ridden his motorcycle the entire twelve hours (overnight!) just so we could see each other. The landlord had let him in after confirming who he was. I thanked him and jumped in my Honda and drove over from the Harvard campus. We spent the day together after he woke up. He met my boyfriend, and then he left the next morning, as he was shipping back out to the DMZ in about a month after his leave. My brother rode from North Carolina to Boston on a motorcycle just to see me!

It was the last time we would see each other while he was alive.

He rode to Texas around Easter in 1993, traded in his old bike, got a new one, and rode back to base after visiting everyone in the family in Austin and Houston. Looking back, it was like he was on a goodbye tour with our Texas relatives. Then he drove to Myrtle Beach with a few other soldiers before they shipped out. His bike hit a pothole, and he lost control and crashed. He died on April 18, 1993.

I remember our last conversation when he said that he would call me later that evening, but when the phone rang, it was my parents telling me that soldiers had arrived at their door with a flag. I would never hear his voice again. I thought nothing could ever hurt as much.

At the wake, I remember seeing the grease under his thumbnail from working on his bike. After the funeral, I opened my mail and saw the canceled check for $1,000, which helped him finish the down payment for the motorcycle. Another wave of grief washed over me, and I blamed myself.

One week after my brother died, his belongings had still not been returned, and my return-to-work deadline was fast approaching. I called a classmate from Austin High who was a graduate of West Point and asked him to help get my brother's things, as the Army kept giving us the run-around. Within hours, my brother's trunk of belongings was located, and a tracking number was given. I flew back to Boston the next day.

My then-boyfriend was clueless, but I thought his family was kind during that time. But their kindness was performative, as I realized later. I also realized that no one could ever understand the pain of a sudden loss unless they had been through it themselves.

After the funeral, my boyfriend said a few naïve things and engaged in some actions, including infidelity, that changed my trust. Then his actions around another familial matter made me realize that young love can burn out and is rarely meant to be forever.

He told me that his family did not approve of me because I was from a "working class" family, and they were more "pedigreed." His father had told him they were "better than our family." He may have felt that it was right to share those thoughts, but in the end, it was hurtful, and it changed my view of his family.

Their thoughts did not make me shrivel up, but instead provided rocket fuel for focusing on my goals. Someone telling you that you are "not good enough" is just another moment to comb the cotton to get the debris out—to become a better you.

The president of the consulting firm, Jim Down, called me. He said that he was so sad that I had lost my brother, and that he understood. I didn't ask how he understood, but his kindness was action-oriented. He simply said, "Every day you will get up, you will get dressed, and you will come into the office. You will stop by my office to say hello to me or to my assistant. And if you can stay to do an assignment, that is good, but if you need to get back home to cry or grieve, it is okay."

He continued, "After three months, I want you to come tell me what you want to do, and let's get you back on track. In the meantime, find a grief counselor so that you can get back to being you."

Work became my constant. I leaned in so far that life disappeared. Never wanting to be hurt again, I pushed close relationships away after breaking up with my boyfriend, as he had returned to Texas, and I did not wish to return with him, which was the condition if we continued our relationship.

I found a grief counselor and decided to always walk to her office, even though it was over a mile away. It forced me to think. She taught me that sudden loss can create an irrational fear of abandonment, harm, and loss, and cause quick attachments. I wish that I had leaned further into therapy so that I could really understand that energy, as I might have had different personal relationships after the loss of my brother.

And I cried. And cried. And cried. Until my tear ducts froze. And I have never been able to cry tears profusely again.

After three months, I knew that the consulting firm role was not the right job for me, but I still wanted to stay in the Northeast.

I went to Jim's office, and he was so kind to always ask me, "How are you?" I told him that I was better, and then he asked, "Did you think about your next steps? Do you want to stay here or transition away? How can I help?"

I said, "No, I don't want to stay at this firm, but I am so grateful to you. It means a lot that you allowed me to figure it out, so that I didn't just run back to Texas. I have been seeing a grief counselor, and she kept hearing a theme about me wanting to help people. But I don't know how I can do that in a for-profit?"

He chuckled. "Robin, you have expensive tastes, and not-for-profit is likely not the right direction. But since you like to help people, have you ever heard of headhunters? Executive recruiters? I think you would be great at that profession. Take a few days to think about how I can help you get into that field with an introduction."

Within weeks, I was on the path to a new corporate career trajectory—joining as a vice president at a boutique executive search firm focused on the nonprofit and educational sector. Soon, the Boston Organizing Committee under Rikk Larsen asked for an executive partner. The boutique search firm sponsored me as a liaison/lobbyist for the role during the Boston Olympic bid, where it was amazing to meet so many local business and national political leaders. And the search firm benefited by getting their name in front of business leaders who were grateful for their "contribution" to the Olympic bid cause.

By 1996, within three years of my brother's death, I had leaned into work so much that I was recruited to join a leading Boston publishing house to recruit their executive team leadership. Using money inherited as a beneficiary of my brother's life insurance, I bought a condo in Cambridge with a view of Boston from the roof. I joined the YWCA Board in Boston.

I continued to go to the grief counselor to manage the emotions from the sudden loss, but only on a monthly basis. One afternoon, I told my grief counselor that I thought it might be time to leave Boston—it was too cold, and I felt so lonely.

She told me that one of her friends worked at a search firm with a Boston and New York office, and they just might be looking for someone. I had an interview the next week and got the job as an associate at the Boston office of Heidrick & Struggles. It was certainly a demotion in title (from vice president!), but this global firm was planning to transfer me to the New York City office. Within two months, the transfer came, and it was time to start a new chapter.

Moving to New York started with renting out my condo to Harvard professors. I then said goodbye at an event held at the African Meeting House, and was honored by so many who attended and those who had helped me on my journey through Boston. One attendee said that it felt like a eulogy. It is rare to hear the accolades and kind words that people feel for you while you are still alive. I remain honored by that wonderful evening of tributes on Beacon Hill. Another pass of the comb.

New York was in the midst of a Disney-ification of Times Square. A new Toys "R" Us with a Ferris wheel and a general cleanup of the city made me less fearful during my move. My sublet was located on 48th Street between 2nd and 3rd, in the building with the chessboard on the side. It was only two blocks from the Heidrick & Struggles offices. I transferred to be on the board of the NYC YWCA. There were many introductions through that organization, so plenty of doors opened.

When I joined the Heidrick & Struggles office in 1999, I became the first Black professional in the New York office. There was not another person of color on the floor; not a mail clerk, receptionist, or HR person—and there was one associate who actually came up to me and said, "There has never been a colored person who worked here before." He looked to see if there would be a reaction, but I just made my face go expressionless and said nothing, while continuing to look at him intently until he blushed and mumbled something before fleeing. That was our last interaction. He was fired shortly after for saying something provocative to a female partner . . . *karma*!

I stayed and began to work for the global managing director of the financial services practice—in layman's terms, he was one of the top people who determined the chess moves for the Wall Street executives and bankers. Almost any time he called or set a lunch, there was a quick confirmation.

I learned about the unwritten rules right away: Making money, maintaining discretion, and access to power are more important than the school one attended. The questions in New York were different from those in Boston. Often it was, "For which firm do you work?" or "What do you do?", and depending on the response, their eyes would either engage or glaze over. Transactional interactions guided friendships as the modus operandi in New York, not pedigree.

This was perfect for someone from Texas, a graduate of the "Ivy of the South." Just saying the words "I'm at Heidrick" was an instant door-opener. I also learned to advocate for myself and to ask for what I was worth.

One day, I asked my new boss, "Why am I paid less than even the junior research team members?"

"Why do you say that? How do you know? How did you find out?" my boss responded. As one would say in poker, his tell was the last question. I knew it was true.

"I learned during an evening out, and someone on the research team said what they earned. And others at my level chuckled and said that this person needed to wait a few more years to earn what the associates earn. But I actually make less than that person, and that means I make less than all the associates. And yet, I am working for you—the top partner—every night until midnight, and they have a social life and leave by seven to go out together," I responded.

He looked at me quizzically. I went silent—and met his eye. A trick learned is the "pregnant pause" to allow someone else to talk.

I got the raise. A few days later, the associates were called into an office meeting and reprimanded to "refrain from discussing salaries" as it is not anyone else's business. Thank goodness I learned about this salary discrepancy before that meeting.

My boss became a mentor to me, and his family welcomed me into their home since I had no real family in the Northeast. I remain forever grateful to them for their kindness.

But he was tough, and the lesson of a lifetime would come less than two years later, when he almost fell off his chair doubled over in laughter.

Mentors vs. sponsors vs. advocates. Mentors will hear you as you formulate your strategy and give advice, but it is up to you to figure out the nuances to reach your goal. A sponsor will guide you to the door, open it, and, with wisdom and input, introduce you to those on the other side. A mentor points you to the door, while a sponsor opens the door and helps you walk through it. And an advocate speaks highly of you, even when you are not in the room.

"It's been a week," he said, "and you still haven't signed the f*cking papers." The *papers* he was referring to were sitting on my desk and had been given to me a few weeks prior, after the company signaled that they were going to go public. "*Those* papers," he emphasized, indicating a pile on my desk.

I casually shrugged my shoulders. "I haven't looked," I said, "but I'm not interested in an HMO. I have health insurance already."

He looked puzzled. "Interested in a *what*?"

"An HMO. I already have health insurance," I stressed.

That's when my boss doubled over laughing. He laughed so hard, he had to sit in the chair, and then he doubled over and almost fell out of the chair. His loud guffaws drew the attention of others who peeked into the door. If I had been a fairer shade, I would have been blushing as I felt my ears get warm. Why was he laughing at me?

"Oh my god," he said, "that's the funniest thing I've ever heard. This is not about an HMO. These papers are for our initial public offering. An IPO. They're for when our company goes public, and you acquire shares based on how long you've been working here. You are about to get paid! This is not about health insurance!"

I felt the heat rise in my face again (a moment to be grateful for my brown skin!) and still did not fully understand but was far too embarrassed by my lack of knowledge.

"This company is going to continue to grow," my boss continued. "Those shares that you thought were HMOs are going to be worth a bit more than you realize. They're all yours, and I'll explain later, but for now . . . sign the f*cking papers!"

I signed the papers, and wouldn't you know, my boss was right. The company received a windfall valuation and increased interest once it went public. Despite the money I'd stand to earn down the line if I stayed, I was thinking about applying to a graduate program at NYU or Columbia and had taken my GRE test.

I didn't know what I wanted to do, but it'd been a dream of mine to earn a master's degree—attribute it to the importance my Texan parents had placed on education. I had a choice to make: Would I stay in a navy-blue-suit job and get paid handily in the process, or would I follow some starry-eyed plan to attain a graduate degree? It was a pivotal moment.

But I could. I would. I had a plan. I knew that if I told him I would use the profit from my divestment to pay for grad school, he would be less inclined to make me feel bad about it.

The next afternoon, after the stock announcement had been made and the partners returned from ringing the bell, I rode the elevator down to the first floor, crossed the street, and entered a global bank with an appointment made after signing the IPO papers. Fighting any instinct to make "secure money," I entered the domain of a sponsor and took the elevator ride up to his offices, which was the start of my real entrepreneurial future—asking for professional and personal advice.

"Hey, kid, you are rich now. How does it feel?" he said with a wide mustachioed smile.

I shook my head. "I don't know. It's a bit surreal, but I do know that this might be a good time to make a change. I just don't know how to get there," I said.

Immediately, he saw that I was stuck. "What's your passion?" he questioned. Nobody had ever asked me that before, so I didn't know how to answer. When he saw that my ambitions were stretching beyond the confines of a corner office and a need to zigzag rather than climb a straight line up the corporate ladder, he asked me what I wanted to do.

I didn't understand what he meant at first because no one

had ever asked me that question. It had always been about getting a job, not chasing a dream. My parents had been supportive, but strategic decisions were not in place. It was almost a spaghetti factory approach—throw it at the wall and see what sticks.

When I couldn't answer his straightforward question, he pivoted. He said, "Put it this way. When you open *The New York Times* on the weekend, which section do you flip to first?"

"Real Estate," I quickly responded.

"I didn't expect that. I thought you might say Style or Weddings. And why is that?" he asked.

"My parents have real estate, and one day I'm set to inherit property, and I want to know strategies for how to go about maximizing value when or if the time comes."

He responded, "I get it. That's a good reason. Let's talk about that. Now I want to know what type of person you are—how do you think? Do you like practical or theoretical?"

I raised my eyebrow.

He explained. There were two graduate real estate programs he respected: NYU and Columbia. He believed that the NYU program was practical, where you would actually develop a property as your thesis. Columbia was more about the theoretical approach to real estate. He wanted to know which curriculum would appeal to me.

He realized I was at a nexus in the road when I was working at the executive search firm.

Though a corporate man himself, he understood the monotonous routine of smile and dial, research, play politics, receive a promotion, and wear the corporate uniform. I had been part of the team that had recruited him to this global bank (and negotiated a salary ten-times higher!), and as an economist, he understood the post-IPO reality. He told me that one day the stock price would drop as soon as the partners were able to cash out. He wanted me to make a good decision about my shares. He was a true sponsor who could see around the corner and was trying to save me from a disappointing realization down the line.

After he explained this, he helped me by opening the door, picking up the phone, and asking, "What are your GRE scores?" I told him. "Okay, let me make a call." He dialed his desk phone, spoke to someone, and a moment later, a fax machine began to whir, and his assistant brought in a NYU application. He asked me to complete it and then wrote a letter of reference.

Then he told me how I was going to have to navigate selling my stock to maintain my references. He said it must be clear that I was selling my stock to pay for graduate school instead of taking loans. But he warned me that when (*not if!*) partners learned that I had sold my stock, they would try to bully me to maintain my holdings and would threaten to fire me. He said that if they learned that I was paying for graduate school, they might back off. I should propose working during the day and going to school at night to ensure they understood that I still believed in the firm. Plus it would ensure that I would have money to actually develop my real estate project in the future.

Then he explained the real reason they would be upset: The firm valuation is based on the "talent," and in a professional services firm, the "talent" leaves by elevator each night. His counsel was that the partners were "locked up" and could not sell during a certain time period. But when the lock-up period ended and they could sell, the stock price would decrease since the partners would sell their shares, retire, or start competing firms. (And a few years later, that is exactly what happened! The valuation decreased.) He was very clear: This was my chance to use a windfall to go to graduate school.

That day, I sold the stock. And the very next day, two partners plus my boss came in to confront me. "Not an option," my boss said when I told him I was considering going to grad school. "You can't leave now. You shouldn't sell your shares." I told them that my intent was to remain at the firm, and my plan was to work during the day and go to school at night. And my family was excited, and this was the only way that I could afford to attend. With reluctance, they left my office, but they were less upset and made me promise not to tell the other associates that I had sold my shares. And my boss turned around and said these words: "This better not affect your work."

Years later, in 2024, I was named a Distinguished Alumnus for the NYU School of Professional Studies and gave the convocation speech to graduate students at Radio City Music Hall!

My mentor-sponsor references and a call opened the door to NYU. With my GRE scores and application, I was accepted. With candles burning at both ends with work and studying, I kicked the door down on graduate school, and three years later, I had a master's degree focused on real estate development so that now I knew that it was possible to *actually build doors*! On graduation day, both my parents attended, and with tears in our eyes, we held hands afterward and looked to the heavens . . . part of a dream with my brother had come true!

QUESTIONS TO COMB THROUGH

1. How have you navigated a tough choice to chase your dreams, even if it was contrary to others' wishes, such as moving to another city or selling off stock?
2. Have you ever been told you or your background is not good enough?
3. Have you reached back to pull someone up with guidance or funding? Or has someone who believed in you passed away before they could see your progress toward your dream?

Chapter 9

Combing Cotton

Cotton gin machines use long combs to separate the cotton fibers (lint) from the seeds, removing other debris and impurities. The combed cotton is then packaged and prepared for processing and transformation.

It was a few weeks after September 11, 2001, and the acrid smell still permeated downtown. We walked through the kitchen into the restaurant, as we rarely used front doors. After greetings, we sat down. He was seated between Granny and me, with Dad on the other side of Granny and Mom on my right.

He and Granny got into an animated conversation about

travels and children. He was always perfectly charming. When I tuned back in, I heard:

"I had six children," said Granny.

As he held my hand, he responded, "I have five children, and I love my kids!"

Mom and Dad were highly amused because Granny spoke to him like she would anyone in her wide-ranging conversation. He was just a nice man who was dating her granddaughter. She called him a "young man," and he thought that was funny. Although he was a widely recognized actor, she did not recognize him—as she never watched R-rated movies and never went to the movie theaters, except for cartoon "pictures" with her grandchildren.

Then he turned his attention to my dad. They started speaking about movies, specifically "A Bronx Tale," where he spoke to Dad about getting his commercial license and learning to drive a bus. Then they began a long conversation about other subjects. I spoke to my mom for a while, and when I turned back, he and my dad were discussing a recent movie, "Men of Honor." It made my dad emotional when he watched it because he thought about his eldest brother, who served in WWII, and they shared stories.

After the food arrived, there was a happy energy at the table. We were having a nice dinner, until someone in the restaurant tipped off the paparazzi, and the scrum appeared at the front door. My boyfriend gave me that look and said to my parents, "So nice to meet you, but we have to go now. A car is waiting for you at the front and will take you back to the hotel when you are done. In the meantime, Robin and I are going to exit through the kitchen, and we'll meet up with you later. Are you comfortable at the Tribeca Grand Hotel? Let me know if you need anything. So nice to meet you." He reached down to hug my Granny, and she beamed. He shook Dad's hand and hugged my mom. Dad offered to pay, but my boyfriend told him that it was already taken care of and suggested a dessert.

We walked through the kitchen to an alleyway, where another car was discreetly waiting on the side street. We jumped in before the photographers knew we had departed. The car drove us around the corner to his home at 110 Hudson Street, where we talked for a while. I asked him if it was okay for me to use the SUV the next day, as I wanted to take my parents and Granny to the Guggenheim and drive around to see a few other spots in the city. He said he would make sure the car was ready and said that he enjoyed talking to my Granny and meeting my parents. He told me to take the elevator to the top of the Guggenheim so that we could wheel Granny down, instead of up, the rotunda. Great suggestion!

When Mom called to say that they had returned to their rooms at the Tribeca Grand Hotel, I walked over to say good night and to confirm our plans for the next day.

Granny said, "That young man was very nice. He looked really familiar. I enjoyed talking to him. I like him. He seems like he is really nice to you."

By the time he met my family, we had been dating for around a year. My parents commented on the acrid smell in the air from the collapsed World Trade Center, where workers with bright lights worked around the clock to comb the debris before removal.

After my parents returned to Texas, my boyfriend and his assistant asked me to walk through a few apartment buildings to see what I thought about the options. I liked the Langham rental unit at 135 Central Park West with the views over the park. He wanted to move uptown because he was concerned about air quality and the health of his children. He did not believe the EPA officials who said that the air was safe, so a move uptown was deemed best, while the downtown unit was being renovated—and I worked with a designer to create a look book, select materials, and start the coordination of the loft that would ultimately be sold.

At the same time, he and his business partners were focused on ensuring that the first responders and the downtown community remained vibrant, so they devised the Tribeca Film Festival as a cultural destination. My sole contribution to the conversation was a suggestion that they rescue a vintage carousel to create a venue for children.

During the inaugural festival, I was flown to Texas to go to the Lake Austin Spa Resort, so that I could relax. While it hurt my feelings at the time, today I understand his logic to keep his personal life separate from his business, "in case we did not work out."

In 2000, we met through a matchmaker who was featured in a *New York* magazine article where she said that she wanted to match one of her clients who was looking for a smart, beautiful Black woman. I got in touch through the writer, and after the yenta interviewed me, background checked me, and asked me a litany of personal questions, she said that she would introduce me to this bachelor.

At first, she would not tell me who he was and only said he was a celebrity. But then she said he had five children. I asked her if he was a widower. She just smiled and said, "No, it's complicated. But he does have caregivers, so you would not have that burden. And he is a very private, shy, funny, smart person."

I told her that I was not just going to meet a stranger, and she at least had to give me their first name. She said his full name. I paused, and my response was, "Why would he need to work with you?"

She said, "He wants to meet someone special. He has been separated from his wife for the past two or three years, and he wants someone who can be around his family. He wants to be married again and is in the process of a divorce. And do you really think he can just go to a bar and meet people?"

I nodded with understanding. We concluded our meeting with a firm handshake, and she said that someone would be in touch. It felt almost like a go-see from modeling days.

The next morning, the phone rang at 7:30 AM. It was Halloween 2000.

"Hello," I said as I moved *The New York Times* away from my lap on the small sofa in my rent-stabilized studio above the Silver Star Diner at 65th and 2nd Avenue.

A man's voice. Nervous, shy, soft-spoken. He said, "Hi . . . uh . . . Robin. Did I wake you? Um, what are you doing?" as he heard the rustling of the paper.

"Oh, I was reading *The New York Times*," I responded.

"Oh, wow. That's nice. You must be smart. Um, Janis told me that you would be expecting my call . . . Um. Can we meet? Are you available later tonight?"

Politely, I responded, "I can't tonight, umm . . . it's Halloween, and I have some plans. It would be better tomorrow."

It was clear that he did not expect me to decline. He didn't know what to say.

So I continued, "I look forward to meeting you."

"Oh yeah, it's Halloween. Okay, my assistant will call you to arrange everything. I look forward to meeting you." He went on to explain that the matchmaker had said good things about me.

With that first phone call and our first meeting at the Bubble Lounge in the private back room, my life changed. He was so kind, very involved politically in the outcome of the "hanging chads," and made me feel special, albeit with some level of complication due to his circumstances.

Upon reflection, this very private man welcomed me into his private world—and he was very thoughtful, with sincerity and moments of laughter. He made it a habit for the years we were together to always wake me up around 7 AM to say "Good morning" from wherever he was working in the world. I thought we were exclusive . . .

I tried to give back in a few ways by helping with the costs in his multiple homes. I suggested that anything that was flushed should be bought by his team at Costco, so they started shopping there for disposable items (e.g., toothpaste, toilet paper, paper towels, soap) because it was less expensive than the nearby NYC bodega. I suggested that he treat his homes like a mini boutique hotel to get cost savings by buying in bulk wholesale.

I did a few special things just for him, too, like making sure his refrigerator was stocked with healthy favorites like peeled oranges for his morning workout and trying to work with his staff to create variety in the evening meals for the children. When we first met, his refrigerator only held caviar and champagne as he ordered takeout from Nobu for our dinner.

But I soon learned—an institution rarely wants change, and the target is on your back if you point out inefficiencies of the team.

When we met, I was in the process of renovating a two-bedroom condo that I had bought in the West Village, located on Bedford between Barrow and Commerce. He visited the unit, looked to his left, and pointed. He reminisced about a time when he and others shared a flat right down the street during his early acting days. One of our common interests was talking about real estate—and he spoke lovingly of his mother and father and his family.

I fixed and flipped the unit and earned a nice profit. He said he was proud of me for doing it so efficiently and on a budget. Then he asked me to do a small project for his Montauk property.

We traveled, and so much was new to me—helicopters, private jets, yachts, private screenings, amazing restaurants, interesting people, and a fantastic trip to Necker Island to meet Richard Branson and Joan, his wife, who made the best chocolate chip cookies!

It was an exciting world, until one day I read *Page Six* at the country house. I showed him a blurb that said that he was getting back together with his wife and the divorce was not moving forward—and the way he looked at me, I knew that it was not idle gossip.

Thank goodness I never gave up my rent-stabilized studio. It was time to get back to work. I moved back into the studio, finished my last semester at NYU, made a trip to Africa as part of the delegation with Ambassador Andrew Young and George

W. Bush, and then bought a mini loft on East 62nd Street a few months later.

So many "friends" disappeared as that relationship ended, and I soon learned why some say that you can count on one hand (or two!) the people who are true friends. He had always said that there were people who may be around for access, and he was right about so many things and so many people. I was thrilled to meet his children when they were young, and to see that they have done so well.

All things considered, I am happy that he met my Granny and Dad before they passed and that we shared so many things that broadened my horizons, with high-level exposure to real estate, politics, travel, architecture, food, family, business, and film.

My final semester at NYU involved a graduate project thesis, which involved a real deal and not just theory. I found a building in Harlem located at 202–204 West 140th Street. The owner was a woman who would sell it to me for $1 million. It was two buildings that were shells, and I wrote up a development proposal for a total of thirty units for the combined building with a combined courtyard entrance and doorman portal.

I created the pro forma, project memorandum, and zoning calculations with an architect and did the construction improvement analysis. I raised almost all the money but could not get the final $250,000. I shared the project with one team led by an investment banker who I thought was a trusted friend. I asked him to assess the project so that we could develop it.

Later, I learned that they had cut me out of the deal while

telling me that the project was not feasible. Recently, I learned that each unit is selling for over $500,000—which means that after construction, this project may have made more than $10 million.

In other words, I received an A in the class and zero dollars.

My investment banker friend never admitted his deception, but I learned a big lesson about greed and betrayal. Greed is definitely something that makes certain people lose their moral compass. Just like Great Granddaddy said, "You can never do good business with a bad person."

The next guy I dated was separated, and that awful pattern of quick attachment reared its head again. I moved from NYC to Washington, DC, with the only connection being the guy. It felt like a good time to get out of town and get a fresh start, but the reality is he should have just been a rebound guy: fun and done.

But that awful pattern of getting too close too fast revealed itself, and I sold my mini loft to a friend, moved away from NYC, my support network of friends, and tried to replicate my design business in a new town.

Trying to replicate a high-end renovation/design-development business was not possible because I had not calculated that Wall Street salaries were different from K Street salaries. Within months, it was clear that moving had been a bad idea, and my fiscal reserves were being tapped out. I got a consulting gig with an investment bank to do executive recruiting and began to rebuild my bank account.

I also maintained a project manager for my design business

in New York City. I was working around the clock—and realizing that following a guy to a new city was a bad idea *for the second time*! My pivot toward a person cost me a significant amount of money to relocate. I had to go for months without any income until I tapped into connections to get the consulting gig. And the guy I moved for . . . he never asked his connections to help.

But the silver lining is that year, we were invited to Thanksgiving dinner at Maya Angelou's home in North Carolina. We flew down, and I was so nervous because there were so many recognizable faces under the tent. At one point, completely overwhelmed, I went inside, and there she was—regal in a chair, in a room by herself. She beckoned to me and said in that inimitable voice, "Child, come here . . ."

The earth stopped, and my breath caught. I did not see another place to sit in the room, so I sat at her feet. A moment later, Cicely Tyson came into the room and sat on the floor opposite me. I don't think I was able to breathe the entire time.

"Child . . . I want you to know that you were invited into my home, and you are acting like you crashed the party. When someone offers you a seat at the table, take your place. I believe that what you are doing is helping people, and that means that it is not a job, but a calling. You are doing good in the world. Now, I want you to know that you came in with him, but he is not 'the one' . . ." And with that, both Maya and Cicely giggled in the way that aunties do when they *know the truth*.

With that, the spell was broken. When he and I returned to Washington, DC, it was clear to me that I was done, but I had to make a plan to relocate. As one would say: I phoned a friend.

The phone actually rang for me. And a plan revealed itself shortly after the Thanksgiving trip. I received a voicemail from someone on Oprah's team. I thought I was being pranked, so I did not return the call. The next day, the same person called, and I *really* thought it was a prank, so I did not return the call again. Finally, this person said on their message, "I am Adam Glassman, and I work with *O Magazine*. I hope that you are available for an interview, and if you do not call, we will have to call the next person on the list to meet the deadline. My number is . . ." I realized that I needed to pick up a magazine to see if his name was in it. It was, and I was about to miss out on the opportunity of a lifetime because I was not returning a phone call!

I made the call, and we had a wonderful and candid conversation. Lesson learned: Return phone calls, or at least have them screened.

Toward the end of the interview, he asked me, "Why do you call your company WSG Consulting?"

I giggled and said, "If I fail, then no one will know." Expecting that he would giggle conspiratorially, I was surprised at the silence.

Adam then said the most powerful words: "Robin, you have been in business for five years. This is a mark that so many small businesses do not reach. If you are not ready to embrace your success or you do not believe in yourself, then why should we share your story?"

He made me realize that I was making myself small, and it was time to embrace the reality—I was an entrepreneur who had reached the radar of *O Magazine*!

"I do believe in myself and my hard work," I responded.

"Then I think that you need to show me—you have a nice name, and maybe if you put your name in your business, it might make a difference," said Adam. "Show me something different in our next call, and then we can run a story. I will call you tomorrow."

Adam showed me grace, and it was a moment of humility for me. He was right.

Within moments, I made a choice. This was a once-in-a-lifetime opportunity. I spoke to the consulting project team leader and said, "I will be out until the day after tomorrow." I then ran out of the office to go home and start a marathon work session. I never went to sleep.

Overnight, I bought the domain name RobinWilsonHome.com, and the tech team at GoDaddy helped me learn how to build a website. By morning, there was a rudimentary website with some portfolio images, and it looked good enough to present. When the phone rang the next day at 10 AM, "Good morning, Adam!" came out in my bleary voice. I had worked all night, and my new direction was ready to be shared.

"So, what did you decide to do?" asked Adam.

I replied, "Are you at a computer? Can you pull up the website RobinWilsonHome.com, please?" There was a moment of silence and clicks on the keyboard.

"Oh my. This is great. Looks like you leaned in. Like the portfolio and the press clips too. Seems like you are going to lean in to your own brand. I am glad to see this. Okay, we will be running the story, and I assume this is the website that you want it to link to?" said Adam.

"Yes!" I replied. This was a sign from the universe, from Maya Angelou, and from the kindness of Adam. The fact that he would take so much time to guide me meant I had another mentor in my life journey! Maybe he has forgotten about this, but I remain grateful to him!

The final straw with the DC rebound relationship was radio silence for a week after dating for a year. He traveled to Disney with his children and did not tell me. When he got back, I asked, "Why?" His response will never leave me. He replied, "You might have wanted to come." The lack of respect told me everything. Ouch!

When I finally agreed to see him, he walked into my gutted apartment over a week later. I had held a garage sale in my apartment, my lease was broken, and the belongings I was taking were packed for the departure back to NYC the next day. My neighbors bought almost everything, and the last night, I slept on an Aero-Bed since most of the furniture was sold. I kept my captain's desk, and most things were able to fit into a Suburban that I had rented—with clothing sent in advance by FedEx.

It was time to return to New York City to rebuild my business while waiting four months for the publication of the Oprah article with my new eponymous branding: Robin Wilson Home.

I swore that I would never follow a man again unless there was a ring on my finger.

I drove back to New York City in a rainstorm in the rented SUV with a goal to put everything into self-storage around the corner from my old mini loft. My friend who had bought my place had given me permission to stay as long as needed to get on my feet since she used the space as a pied-à-terre and mainly lived elsewhere. When I arrived, I unloaded my clothing boxes and racks and used my old keys to move into my old home, still furnished with my old sofa, dishes, and linens.

Had I not sold it to a dear friend for less than the market would bear, I might not have had a place to stay. Imagine if I had not sold it to her? If greed had been my elixir, then I would not have had a free place to stay for fourteen months. She saved my entrepreneurial dreams by letting me couch surf and pour all my revenue back into my business to rebuild.

After this experience of giving away my power for a boyfriend, I decided that I would act as guys do—many of them just focus. So I made a personal pledge and decided that *business would be my boyfriend for five years*, and I would not date anyone seriously (if at all!). If they did not get the message, then I would have to pivot away. I was not going to waste any more time. I would work nonstop and put in the hours to make my business bigger and better than it was before the eighteen-month distraction in Washington, DC.

And I did, only this time I added a team member to help me, and she was also an investor. We created the A-B-Cs needed for a successful business—attorney, bookkeeper, and cash flow!

Through connections, I was invited on news programs to discuss new eco-friendly innovations in the design world and started getting more notice from the media world, paid speaking events, sponsorships, and corporate partners. It was very nice to work on some high-profile projects to build my portfolio.

But one thing I regret is not understanding that building a brand means building the team, and I tried to do everything to save money. That was a mistake . . . in order to scale your business, you must delegate and create a team around a common mission or goal.

But a few months later, the first Oprah article appeared, and everything changed!

QUESTIONS TO COMB THROUGH

1. Have you ever given away your power in a relationship to try to fit yourself into someone else's life? How did you rediscover yourself?
2. Did you ever sacrifice a profit to do something for a good friend—and see the positive outcome on the other side?
3. Have you ever couch surfed, put everything in storage, and taken the risk to go to your last dollar to chase your entrepreneurial dream or rebuild?

Chapter 10

Processing

> Clean cotton lint is sent from the cotton gin to the textile mills for processing, where fibers are carded, spun, and twisted into yarn or thread. After meeting the quality standards, fibers are categorized, graded, and sold to the textile mills. There are two processes: yarning or spinning. When spinning, cotton fibers are drawn out to maximum length and twisted together to form yarn, which is the foundation of fabric.

The late sports attorney Keven Davis was the "phone a friend" call I made. Before I left DC, we'd spoken by phone, and he'd said, "Bro does not know what a jewel he has. I am glad that you finally realized who you are. I am proud of you. You need to get your a** back to New York so you can do your work. Get back up here and get your business back!"

He welcomed me back with a positive phone call and a requirement that I visit his office within twenty-four hours of my return to get a hug. While driving back to New York City, the Alicia Keys song "Empire State of Mind" was my soundtrack, and after unloading the rental car and taking a shower to soothe my muscles, my first night in my old mini loft was spent adjusting to my old sofa and remembering that it was not my home anymore.

Essentially, I was without a home and couch surfing. With great excitement and feeling the energy of the city, I started the next morning by hopping on the subway to ride down to Wall Street.

Keven's law firm was was based in Seattle, and the New York office had just opened with "standard" furnishings. Keven wanted something unique and gave me my first commission to redesign his office. His firm would pay for it—and while the budget was not huge, he said his celebrity clients would see my work, and he could tell them about my firm. He pulled out two posters of Venus and Serena and asked me to get them framed somewhere with UV-blocking glass. I was grateful for a new project to get back on my feet.

Then he told me to sit down at his desk and turned on a program called *The Secret*, which is about the mindset of successful people. I think it was ninety minutes of insight that changed my views about everything! The premise is to remember that sometimes things happen *for* you, and not *to* you.

Without the right mindset, you will focus on the event, and you might not recognize that the universe has a plan. Keven was a mentor, sponsor, and advocate—and his guidance, introductions, and regular reminders to "get my business to the next level" while always speaking so highly of his other clients, Venus and Serena, let me know that with the right people around you and a mindset focused on positive outcomes, everything is possible!

I walked everywhere in NYC and lost the few pounds I'd gained in DC, which was a more car-focused city. Within weeks, my jawline was more chiseled, and my belly was concave since I only ate one meal a day to save money.

Keven introduced me to my future COO and to my future IMG agent. My agent introduced me to TV executives. And his law firm asked me to curate a gallery exhibition, and we discovered an amazing group of emerging artists including Pat Goodman, Angelo Mariano, and Dick Anthony.

My COO and I tried to be early pioneers in remote work, but the SaaS technology used today was not in place, so it was difficult to move efficiently. She is amazing, and I wish that we were able to partner at that time with the tech of today using our formidable multitasking skills—she, a working mom, wife, and wellness enthusiast with an investment banking background. She helped craft the early brand messaging and brought order to the corporate office. Had we continued to work together, I believe the company would have grown faster and smarter, but commuting in from Connecticut cost so much for parking and tolls—and until I became a parent, there was no understanding of the sanctity of the 3 PM school pickup time.

Working with someone who knows more than you is the *best* situation when you are an entrepreneur. In fact, I have learned that the best thing you can do to build a company is to hire those who are smarter than you in their sector and "fire yourself" from that job. For example: If you hire a great website designer or a marketing person, you can free yourself to do other work.

Working with professionals who can see the potential of your dream means that you can learn, remain the visionary, and build the company with clarity. I so admire her mind and ability to make the company more productive, as she was always combing cotton to make things better!

One of the first things she suggested was that we meet with a public relations team and a production team. Her second suggestion was to find a shared office space so that I could stop working in coffee shops and get out of the mini loft. We rented a shared space with an architect located near the Flatiron Building. A video production team was nearby, so we had a conversation about the brand and vision. They wanted to create a syndicated radio- or webisode-style show to follow our journey. It was so exciting, but it never came to fruition.

The public relations team was hired, and they believed my platform should focus on how to help people navigate the world of wellness and clean spaces to minimize allergic triggers. They loved that we were a pioneer in the space and shared that "going green" was a new marketing term that was being used—and they thought my brand could fit into that niche.

A few weeks later, I was booked onto several of the local and one national morning show, plus radio and print. Looking back, those bleary early mornings were the start of building a brand

and a platform. Each interview helped me hone my messaging because the PR team would provide instant feedback.

Socially, every action taken had to do with the business (remember, my business was my boyfriend), so if I went to a social event, it was because there was an invitation or a partnership set up by the PR team. Often, when an event was over, I would return to the office to finish a project.

Sleeping only four to five hours a night (or less) led some people to remark that they did not know how I was doing it. But it was a muscle developed during college—work hard during the week and sleep hard on the weekends. I actually imposed a monk-like rule on Sundays. Until 4 PM, I wouldn't speak to anyone or use technology. I would only read, write, cook, or walk. I did not watch television or drink alcohol for most of those five years.

What people did not know was that there was no fallback. No safety net. My savings were almost gone, as every penny made was poured back into the business. We built a word-of-mouth clientele for interior design projects and handled approximately eight to twelve projects at a time in the New York City metropolitan area. We paid project managers per project and spent a lot of time running around to manage contractors, until we found our go-to team that did their jobs by following the scope of work, timeline, and communicating well. I was building a brand.

The hard work and sacrifice began to show a return on investment within three years, thanks to invitations to high-profile design events and friendships with movers and shakers in the public arena—and a few of those folks from my actor ex-boyfriend's world began to show up again, but they had already "told me who they were," so their entreaties were kept at arm's length.

However, one day, I was having lunch with friends at Cafe Luxembourg, and in walked an A-list actor friend. When he walked in, you could feel the room do a slight shift and head twirl, and the imperceptible hush of people whispering as they see an A-list celebrity. So of course, I turned my head. During my time dating the famous actor, I had played tennis with this man's wife.

He greeted his friends and was two steps from them. And then he saw me. He stopped.

"Robin, oh my goodness. So good to see you. How are you?" and with great warmth, he opened his arms for a hug, so I stood and was enveloped. "Where have you been? We saw that he went back to her, and my wife and I have wondered about you often. Are you okay?"

I replied, "I went to Washington, DC, a few years ago, and when I returned, I kept my head down and worked to rebuild my business. I'm doing well. How is your family?"

We spoke a moment longer, and he hugged me again. I turned around, and my friends having lunch with me were staring at me like I was an alien. They all stage whispered in unison, "Wait a second. Oh my gosh, Robin! How do you know him?"

I downplayed it by replying, "Oh, he is friends with one of my exes, and it was a lifetime ago. I played tennis with his wife." My expression indicated we should talk about other things, and we tried to get back to our lunch. I did notice that suddenly our waiter became much nicer!

QUESTIONS TO COMB THROUGH

1. Have you ever done a focused review of your life and made steps toward an intentional pivot?
2. Have you ever run into someone from your past and realized how far you have come?
3. With today's technology, do you understand how efficiently you can create a virtual team to work with you to build your company?

Part 3

Purpose

Chapter 11

Branding

Cotton is classed for quality attributes. Sometimes, quality attributes like staple length can define the branding, such as Supima®, Egyptian, or Giza, for quality. Once defined, the marketplace can place a premium because of strength, softness, or fibers.

The earth shifted when the phone rang. You never forget that phone call where the only answer is "YES!"—and at that moment, as my paternal grandmother would say, you have entered "high cotton," as your entire existence is about the shift.

The receptionist in my studio answered the phone and told me that a woman named Amanda was asking for me, and then added, "She has a real Southern drawl."

"Hello, this is Robin," I said into my phone.

"Hi, I'm Amanda, and you were recommended to me by

Laura Turner Seydel in Atlanta. She is a leading environmentalist. She said you are a leading green designer. Are you taking design clients? If you are available, my client asked that you visit their residence tomorrow."

I responded: "Is it in Atlanta? Can you tell me more about the project?"

She replied, "It is in upstate New York, Westchester County. And the client is Mary Richardson Kennedy and Bobby Kennedy Jr., and they have a home that was completely overrun with black mold. They are mostly through the demolition now, and they are staying around the corner at a rental. But I need to bring on a designer who understands eco-friendly options and who can help them through the furnishing and media coverage. We researched and found you. And everyone we spoke with says that you are able to also project manage a renovation. Can you make yourself available on short notice? I need to confirm with them today that you can be there tomorrow. If they like you, you will be hired immediately for the project."

My head spun as I heard the Kennedy name. In my mind, I was jumping for joy.

My voice did not betray the excitement. "Yes. Of course. I will clear my calendar," I said as I beckoned to the receptionist across the room, who immediately picked up her phone to cancel and reschedule appointments. Writing the details on a Post-it Note and doing a quick Google search while still holding the phone against my neck, it was clear that yes, it *was* the Kennedy family and that Laura—who had recommended me—was the daughter of Ted Turner, who founded CNN.

My expression must have been stunned because three team members crowded around my desk. When I hung up and told them, we all danced around the studio. Then we got serious.

What did I need to bring? Should I bring a team member? How long was the drive? We all agreed that the first meeting should only be me driving a Zipcar upstate.

Everything in my personal and professional life had prepared me for this moment. It was so powerful to realize that:

- My pan-allergic childhood had helped me understand allergic triggers.
- My internship at LCRA had taught me to be organized with voluminous data.
- My summer internship in San Francisco had placed me around immense wealth.
- Modeling had taught me how to walk into a room and always be on time.
- Executive search had taught me the immense power of discretion.
- Dating a celebrity had taught me to listen first before offering solutions.
- Couch surfing taught me to be frugal.
- Being an entrepreneur (at that time it was ten years!) had taught me the premise of being ready to take advantage of an opportunity.
- Being around the right people focused on success had taught me to just "accept my seat at the table" and not to question why I was called—and to know my worth!

In fact, in executive search, we had to sign a pledge to maintain confidentiality on high-level searches because leaked information could move the stock market. We often knew things before *Bloomberg* or *The Wall Street Journal*.

In the future, when you read a news headline that a CEO is leaving a company to spend more time with family, and the same day a replacement comes from an outside company, then you know that a recruiter was handling that search behind the scenes for months. And likely a pre-agreed press release was crafted as part of the exit strategy to ensure a smooth transition and to ensure the stock price remains stable. Working with Fortune 500 companies and their boards of directors means being privy to a chess match of people moving their careers around the global stage.

Similarly, as a designer of celebrity homes, the private domain of someone's residence must be treated with the same level of discretion—budgets, personal preferences, and private details of a person's life must never be disclosed unless a high-profile client tells you that they want publicity (e.g., magazine exposure). If they prize discretion, the public may never know the names of our clients. Especially those who have multiple spaces—as they must ensure security is maintained for their family and residence.

Many people think that wealthy individuals prize money, but the reality is that they prize relationships and time, which are priceless. And they strive to be surrounded by intellectually curious people who "know how to get things done" or who have valuable connections—and they hire professionals with a similar mindset. My clients knew that I respected their time and budgets, and they hired our team because we "get it done" as the owners' rep on the construction side, and then pivoting to the design side to furnish their home—to create a sacred space.

So many of these individuals share their time in a public sphere, and when they have off time, they want to feel comfortable with their friends and family, and with colleagues who have earned a place in their private lives.

Over time, both designers and architects come to know things about their clients by watching the dynamics between a couple, knowing what is in their drawers, or noticing clues like a primary suite with two bedrooms or that all fiscal details are handled by the business manager, leaving design decision-making to our team with only early input when the client is traveling and simply wants to view the finished product. At the end of the day, our goal is to create a home for them, no matter their situation, taste, or budget. Simple details like remembering if someone is right-handed or left-handed can ensure that we design in a way that feels natural for them in their space. Details make all the difference.

The Kennedy project lasted for two years, and we made decisions with input from our client about every item in the entire home. Sometimes we selected vendors, and sometimes items were donated from leading companies and brands in exchange for publicity. My branded line of kitchen cabinetry was selected for the residence—which made a multi-page spread in *House Beautiful* for "Kitchen of the Month" in May 2010. At the same time, I began to use the commuter train to Westchester instead of driving a Zipcar every time and broke the keys on two BlackBerry devices while typing out my pre-approved book concurrent to the project.

At the same time, my team and I managed around ten other clients each year, so the office was quite busy consulting with developers and clients in New York, Seattle, California, Florida, and Texas, plus a few hospitality room setups and lobby projects across the country.

Simultaneously, I hired someone to build a new website, with a focus on my clean design protocol. The new site guided consumers with tips (blog), products (online shop), and interiors (design), and there was more content to add after my news appearances on Fox, ABC, NBC, CBS, PBS, and in print. It was day by day, and we began to realize that an eponymous brand was truly developing!

A few more appearances in the pages of *O Magazine*, plus several paid speaking events, allowed my business to see revenue growth. And for the first time in almost four years, I actually paid myself on a regular basis, and I moved out of my friend's pied-à-terre and found a shared loft space within four blocks of my Flatiron office, near the Empire State Building. It was easier to work until 3 AM and then walk six blocks instead of walking thirty blocks to my old mini loft in the East 60s. After a few months, I found a large studio apartment on the thirty-third floor (at helicopter level!) located on the East River near The Water Club, so I was still able to walk to our new showroom space at 230 Fifth Avenue.

My interior design business also began to be known for relatively quick kitchen renovations. At some point, we identified an upstate kitchen dealer who was attentive to my clients. By doing a day trip and driving to their Rockland County location, my clients saved around 50 percent off their kitchen cabinets compared to the prices charged in New York City.

We brought so many clients to his shop that he was breaking sales records for his manufacturing partner. After a few months, the CEO of the manufacturer asked the local kitchen dealer what had changed in his business. He said two words: Robin Wilson. The conversions were growing so quickly and exponentially that the CEO asked to meet me, so they flew me and one of my team members to their factory.

We landed in Chicago, and the car drove to Wisconsin—farther and farther from urban areas. At one point, I looked over and saw a frozen lake with a tent and a pickup truck parked on the ice. And then another lake with a tent and a snowmobile. Mesmerized, I finally asked the driver, "What is that? Is that really ice? Cars parked on ice?"

The driver chuckled, "Yes, it is much colder here than down in Chicago. And those are fishermen. They are ice fishing."

"You mean the ice is thick enough for the cars to park on top?"

He replied, "Yeah, it has been this cold for weeks, and they test it before they drive the trucks out. The ones with snowmobiles mean they are not sure if the ice would support the weight of a truck." I didn't say much more except to marvel at how many lakes and fishing tents I saw.

When we arrived in the factory town, it was so nice to see a "Welcome" sign with my name on it at the hotel: "Welcome Robin Wilson." Small-town hospitality is always so amazing!

The next day was a factory tour. Walking through any factory requires awareness of safety and respect for the hardworking people and machines that make it run. A kitchen cabinet factory has so many tradespeople—painters, carpenters, millworkers, machinists, lumbermen, packagers, drivers—and each one is uniquely able to ensure that the cabinets arrive properly at our client projects.

I marveled at the "Made in the USA" pride—flags everywhere and robots mixed in with hardworking people. So many loyal and longtime employees on the factory floor spoke about how they were the second or third generation to work at the factory. Country music was playing on the speakers, and I started to sing along—and someone looked at me, befuddled. They actually asked me, "How do you know this song?"

I responded, "I'm from Texas. This is music that I grew up with." When the next song came on, I knew those lyrics too! Word traveled quickly, and warmth exuded from everyone on the factory floor because I wasn't just a "big-city designer," but a warm-blooded American who respected these folks who were just earning an honest living while making quality "Made in America" cabinetry products for over four hundred independent kitchen dealers.

They took me to the end of the line, and I saw a box exiting the firing kiln, and they said that it was one from my client's order—and in a few days, that order would head east. It was thrilling!

After the tour, we entered a conference room, and the business meeting began.

The then-CEO said, "We would like to license your brand, and given the sales numbers generated, we think that you could help as an ambassador for a specific product line. Here are the terms if you wish to work with us to license your brand." He handed me some papers. "If we can come to an agreement, we look forward to visiting your studio in New York."

The rest of the conversation was routine, and the excitement in the room was palpable, but I was cool as a cucumber. They were trying to sell me on this business idea of licensing, but what they did not know was that *I had no idea what licensing was*—and I needed to speak with a trusted advisor to really understand. They thought I was tepid about the idea, so they actually added a percentage to the royalty. This was my first licensing deal opportunity!

Smiling, I responded, "I am very excited and will read everything on the plane. Our team will come back to you very quickly. Love your factory and love the energy of your team. They obviously take such great pride in their work, and it is so exciting to hear the story of how this family-run business, since the 1930s, has grown. Now, I am starving and haven't eaten since I left New York at 6 AM this morning." Everyone chuckled.

They took me to a local restaurant with the senior management team, and it was the first time that I saw cheese curds on the menu as an appetizer. I don't remember if I tried that dish, but I do know that everything was delicious!

After dinner, they took me to the hotel. Before going to sleep that night, I faxed the offer to our corporate counsel and spoke briefly with them about the deal. Although I did not fully understand, he was excited. Then he explained the magnitude of this opportunity. For the first time, my brand was coming into clarity, and I realized that all the sacrifices and hard work were coming to fruition. Processing details behind the scenes was our team of attorneys, who worked through the week to do red-line markups until everyone was satisfied and the documents were ready to sign.

A few weeks later, the manufacturing firm's CEO and senior leadership came to New York, along with the local kitchen dealer to whom we had brought so much business. They visited my showroom at 230 Fifth Avenue, and I handed over my signed contract. The CEO countersigned, and after a ceremonial handshake, we had a deal.

Our time in person was to ensure that we bonded, and they marveled that you could see the Empire State Building from our design studio window. Then we went up to the roof deck, and they walked around the perimeter to look at the city and New Jersey at dusk.

From there, I took them to get a little bit of Texas in New York at my favorite BBQ joint right around the corner—Hill Country Barbecue Market. One of the owners was there, and he pulled out all the stops, reserving a section of the restaurant and pulling out silver trays piled high with every type of meat: short ribs, sausage, brisket, chicken, and every side, plus dessert after we finished. There was also country music playing with a live band! We all felt right at home.

We had survived the economic downturn that started in 2008, but I realized that there were many times as an entrepreneur that I was paying my team and not myself. Some of the team members were not pulling their weight. So after lowering our headcount, we moved to a new showroom space a few blocks away at 7 West 34th Street, across from the Empire State Building. It was closer to my residence and much less expensive.

My team set up the showroom to mimic a living space, with a bed, linens, and other items, so that we could show what the brand could be if other licensing deals were made. In hindsight, we should have moved into one of the NYC design buildings. We actually had conversations for a showroom in the New York Design Center, on Lexington Avenue in the 30s, but we could not come to an agreement on rent, so we declined. In retrospect, that was a mistake. Had we moved into the design center, we might have had broader brand name recognition, and our clients could have shopped other showrooms easily. It may have made the brand grow more efficiently, and so many amazing brands are in that building now! Oh well.

Lesson learned: Without a plan, you don't understand where you are going. Upon reflection, avoid all penny-wise and pound-foolish moments if possible.

Christmas 2008 was the rebuilding phase for the company. We had laid off those who were not performing, signed a licensing deal, and hit a milestone for revenue, knowing that the kitchen deal was on the horizon in January and funds would start coming in. Without thinking it through or speaking to the bookkeeper, I paid all the corporate bills down to zero, except our attorney. In the process, I forgot to pay myself.

To celebrate, I threw a holiday party for my team at TAO in Manhattan. Everyone had a great evening and talked about their plans for the week that they were off (with paid leave!), and then it was time to go. I was wearing my cute shoes, cute coat, and a minidress. It was cold! I went next door to the Four Seasons to get funds from the ATM and looked agape at the screen. All I had was $1.23 in my bank account. Not even enough to get a subway token. I exhaled and realized that I had taken care of everyone else and not myself!

"May I get you a cab?" asked the doorman as I exited the lobby.

"Oh no, I am going to walk a few blocks to clear my head. Happy holidays," I said blithely, as though it was a warm winter night with a puff of steam in the frosty air.

I began the trek from 58th Street to the East 30s in my less-than-appropriate clothing and coat. I walked home and started shivering around 40th Street, even with a fast pace, as the wind tunnels between the buildings started to whip now that it was almost 11 PM. My teeth were chattering, and I could not feel my hands when I walked into the lobby of my building.

"Miss Robin, what happened? Are you okay?" the doorman asked with alarm.

"I couldn't get a cab, so I walked home . . . I guess it was colder than I thought," I said to him.

He said, "Ma'am, you must get warm. You look like you are on the edge of frostbite. Don't put any warm water on your hands. Just warm up your bathroom and stay in there until you get warm again. Get some tea. And Merry Christmas," he said.

I felt tears on my cheeks while shivering as the elevator ascended to the thirty-third floor. I was broke. My one credit card was maxed out, and I only had $1.23 in cash. No plan B, no cookie jar, no relatives nearby.

Press releases were out telling everyone that I had a new licensing deal. I had a studio on Fifth Avenue. My company was in good shape, and funds were forthcoming, but I had to make it until after New Year's. But I was not taking care of me. I took care of everyone else. Without shame, I could not ask for any help.

I remember opening my refrigerator, and it was a *Sex and the City* version: a few condiments, a few beverages, eggs (probably rotten), and some old take-out containers. Maybe juice from concentrate would work for breakfast? Or I could go on a fast for a week and just drink water?

My teeth still chattered, and I tried to hop around. But I could not feel my feet and felt unsteady. I turned the heat up to eighty degrees. I turned on the teakettle and realized I did not have any tea bags. Oh well, time for hot water.

The phone rang, and the caller ID said "Mom & Dad."

"Hi, happy holidays," I said as cheerfully as I could muster.

My mom said, "Happy—what is wrong? You sound funny." I could hear Dad saying something in the background.

"Oh, I am just shivering. There were no cabs, and I had to walk home, so I am just getting in. It is so cold. I'm about to boil some water and then try to warm up in the bath," I said.

"Okay. You had me worried for a second. Well, we just want to call to say merry Christmas. We are going to put $500 in your bank account tomorrow," said Mom.

Dad chimed in, "Because we didn't know what to get you, and we are so proud of you for all these *license plate* things that you are doing."

I started to smile, then giggled at his *license plate* comment.

Then I just said, "Thank you, Mom and Dad. I am so grateful." The piercing shriek of the teakettle broke the moment.

The next day, the funds were in the bank by 10 AM. I went to the grocery store and did the responsible thing by buying rice, tuna, cereal, almond milk, eggs, spinach, tortillas, pasta, sauce, and a few other things that could stretch for the next ten days.

That's family for you—intuitively there when you need them.

> My business mantra is A-B-C or 1-2-3. Translated: You need to build your business with a great attorney, bookkeeper, and cash flow, or you will have $1.23 in your pocket.

My five-year pledge to "make my business my boyfriend" was coming to an end. Several of my friends were thrilled that my focus on business goals were coming to fruition, but they all said that if I wanted to have a child, my clock was ticking. The blind dates began. Let's just say that it was interesting to meet different people.

Then some friends vouched for a guy they knew, saying that he was a "nice guy." In July 2011, they introduced us at a reception, and things moved quickly. Because of my religious upbringing, I always felt that I needed to be married to have a child, and he put a ring on it when we got engaged two weeks before my forty-second birthday. We eloped in November, and I was pregnant by January. I brought my daughter home from the hospital on my forty-third birthday.

Right before we got engaged, I once again repeated the pattern of upheaval and moved to New Jersey—moving my life for a guy that I really did not know since we were engaged less than ninety days after meeting. He probably did not care that I ended my apartment lease early (lost my deposit), then downsized the team and closed my NYC studio (lost my deposit), and when I got pregnant, we moved to a house in a gated community (paid $5k for a deposit out of meager funds). I had no vehicle. The isolation from friends challenged me, and dropping off the social circuit challenged my business. For him, he had the same job, car, and lifestyle. For me, it was the start of spending the meager savings that I had built up. Three life-changing events in ten months created complete stress and upheaval in my life.

When I look back, he made no real effort at courtship and did not even help with the move (I made two moves in a few months), and all the business changes (and lost deposits) fell on me. The signs were there about why it would not last, including not being added to his corporate insurance policy, with his status still marked as "single" in company records almost thirty days before our daughter was born, even after nearly a year of marriage.

Three of my mentors gave me advice before the marriage, but unfortunately, I chose to ignore all of their thoughts because "my clock was ticking."

The silver lining: We were blessed to have a healthy child. When people ask, I say the best birthday gift ever was bringing my daughter home on my forty-third birthday! (Side note: One thing I learned from my "geriatric" pregnancy DNA test is that the Irish origin stories are true because my results contained a marker that only Irish people have!)

Due to court requirements, I will not speak about certain

events that occurred during the marriage, save to say that in August 2014, I fled with our almost two-year-old daughter to a safe house apartment in Montclair, New Jersey.

Before I closed the door on the marital home the final time, I made sure to make his bed. Time to move on. Combing the cotton. Our divorce was finalized six months later.

Two years later, in 2016, the court issued a lifetime final restraining order against him due to domestic violence, so we began to parallel parent using a portal called OurFamilyWizard and multiple court motions.

In 2023, I received the Purple Ribbon Award for "Survivor of the Year" for creating Project Lilac, a social justice program that uses a portion of our proceeds to provide sheet sets and other supplies to domestic violence survivors. Sheets are given so that families do not have to sleep on a bare mattress when they flee to a safe house. A highlight was meeting and partnering with Yankees legend Joe Torre and partnering for a year with his Safe at Home Foundation.

Today, my firm continues to quietly provide aid in partnership with several other charitable organizations focused on causes related to children, domestic violence survivors, and the unhoused.

Divorce costs a lot. Emotionally, you grieve the loss of a dream. Fiscally, the only winners are the lawyers who probably see another car, house, or vacation in their future. Socially, the family's community is divided, which causes ripple effects for their children. It is like a seismic reaction, and the aftershocks keep coming unpredictably for a long time.

But I learned that with a weak foundation, the cracks keep getting bigger. It is better for your child to grow up in a non-toxic household, for them to grow up in separate spaces where both parents love them in their own way. It is the best gift for your children, so that they do not see or feel things in a home that is not happy—so that they do not have to take years of therapy to manage what they do not understand.

Resilience is always reminding myself that some things are done *for* you, not *to* you. I remain grateful for my daughter and strive to live each day with a positive outlook. And daily, with meditation and walking, I remind myself of the importance of combing debris out of the cotton boll!

QUESTIONS TO COMB THROUGH

1. How would you handle it if someone had the courage to tell you about domestic violence or abuse? Would you help them, or simply ask them if it was a "love tap"? (Yes, someone asked me that!)
2. Do you have a vision board or bucket list? What is your mindset when great or bad things happen?
3. Have you ever tried a day of silence with no distractions or technology? What do you do and what did you learn about your use of time?

Chapter 12

Weaving and Knitting

Yarn is woven or knitted into raw cotton fabric. Weaving creates the warp and weft. Knitting is the interlocking of loops. Each method creates a unique strength to the fabric. Done poorly, this process can create weak construction and less durable fabric.

I thought that building my business up was the hardest part, but I was wrong—the hardest thing was trying to mitigate the risks from someone with the potential to tear everything down.

About two weeks after I fled, my daughter started preschool, and we celebrated her second birthday with a shared cupcake from The Little Daisy Bakeshop in Montclair, New Jersey. That was all I could afford.

But soon, my brand was threatened. Letters were sent to retail executives, board members, and managers with fake names and addresses from various hotels. The same IP address sent one-star reviews, pulling down our former five-star reviews with repetitive language in the reviews. Postal police and retail security teams got involved, and retailers kept removing the fake reviews, but they were coming in on a daily basis. Soon, the brand was pulled off the shelf at a retailer after sales plummeted due to poor reviews. Because there were fewer online shoppers at the time, it was eventually pulled completely. It felt like the last fifteen years of hard work were useless, and I was heartbroken for the friends and family who had invested. But they were more determined than I to stay the course!

My friends with retail backgrounds shared this with me using their retail experience: "Good. Better. Best. You were *good* enough when you met them. You are *better* now that you have moved on. And you will achieve your *best* now on the rest of this life journey!"

Remember, as an older mom, I'd had a high-risk pregnancy and had closed my NYC studio. Unlike a person working in a corporate role with maternity leave and a steady paycheck, an entrepreneur is faced with dwindling savings when not earning money.

Advice for anyone: If you do not feel welcome in the space in which you live, it is time to leave and create your own home. Remember that a house is four walls, and it is a lot easier to leave with necessities than to try to stay. Find your safe space filled with love.

So I had to return to the grind again—rebuilding my business. I had a plan before fleeing and had been writing my second book from the time my daughter was three months old. My book was published in the fall of 2014, a few weeks after I left. I appeared on MSNBC and other media to discuss *Clean Design: Wellness for Your Lifestyle*—and at one airport, it was thrilling to see the book in all the windows of the Hudson Booksellers airport bookstore!

My pattern in a relationship has always been to follow the guy and to give up my power, which is the way that I was raised in our Christian household. But no one ever mentions the cost of what can happen if your spouse does not champion you. You can lose so much, and post-divorce as an entrepreneur is devastating. You spend hours in courtrooms and prepping days in advance—so the distraction from earning is intense. It was spiritual and psychological warfare.

I had to start over from my 400-square-foot, one-bedroom rental New Jersey apartment instead of my NYC studio on Fifth Avenue across from the Empire State Building. When my legal bills topped $850,000, it heralded a new reality: My savings were gone, my exposure on the design scene was minimal—and there were no pension, benefits, or steady paycheck. I was broke.

An entrepreneur earns and has to pay everyone and every bill before they pay themselves. After they pay everyone else, what is left is their salary, if anything at all. That means that my fifteen years of hard work and sacrifice were now in the bank accounts of attorneys due to court motions and filings. The child support was spent on caregivers, child expenses, rent, and food. Any awards given by the court had to be garnished if not willingly paid, so that by the time it was received, the fees went to the attorneys. I learned that the legal system does not understand the nuances of domestic violence and how motions can exacerbate fiscal abuse.

Christmas 2015. My daughter and I did not have much in the way of material items for Christmas. We bought a little pine tree that was about a foot tall, and I told my daughter that it was a mini tree that was her size! She called it her baby tree, and I was glad that she did not know the difference. We put tinsel on it and a string of popcorn.

Her childlike innocence made everything okay. I rewrapped some toys that she had never played with and made them "new" for her. My parents bought her clothes, and two of her godmothers added to her long-term savings account and gave her new toys and books.

Someone told me to remember that even though I felt like I was getting coal for that holiday, I should remember that diamonds are a piece of coal, and some people don't know the difference. I worked hard, paid bills, saved to buy a house, and recognized that I needed to find a school district with one choice for elementary school since I had primary custody and she would go to the school where we lived.

During this time, the dichotomy was: The world perceived me as successful because I was on and in the news, but the reality was vastly different. The image had been built up over the years, but after thirty-three months of marriage, a single choice to say "yes" made a reality: my business and brand were holding on for dear life.

It made me feel like my entire life was a performance. Acting brave and strong for my daughter, confident in court, yet feeling terrified and alone in quiet moments while counting pennies for bills and borrowing from friends and family.

One memorable moment was paying the attorney, rent, and caregiver, and then having no money left for groceries. The phone rang. My dear friend from Lamaze class, whose husband owned a grocery store, said she wanted to stop by to say hello—and she brought six bags of groceries. I did not have to ask, but my prayers were answered!

Personal pivots occur in friendships, dating, and marriages after you establish strict boundaries in your life about what you will allow. When you push back on the superficial and insist on the basic checklist required—kindness, respect, generosity, and empathy—you will easily identify those who should stay or go from your personal life.

And if you have means or a successful business, you must get a prenuptial agreement to legally set boundaries. And I suggest that you stay with someone for four seasons to let time tell if they should earn a permanent spot in your private life.

Today in my living room, there is a Winnie-the-Pooh lithograph. Piglet asks, "How do you know if you are loved?" and Pooh responds, "You just feel it."

So I worked almost twenty-four hours a day. My mom and two of my daughter's godmothers, Cheryl and Joy, pitched in by coming up from Texas or DC on a regular basis to help. My parents and friends all said to stay focused—reminding me that they believed in me, saying that I was a phoenix who would rise and succeed, reminding me of the positive example I was setting for my daughter.

Due to my lifetime of fragile health, this moment in time took my body to the brink. I was getting ill in a way that foretold a disastrous health outcome: asthma attacks, palpitations, PTSD symptoms. One day, my mother and a friend sat me down. They both said, "You are getting too thin, and we cannot hold this together if you get sick. You must rest more and start to eat. If you are not here, then was it all worth it?"

Focusing entirely on business with three jobs can move the business forward, but it is also like not putting on the oxygen mask first. I was not treating myself well, and with my asthma, the flare-ups pushed me to the point of great harm. I was not in my twenties anymore.

I called this a period of JOB (like the Bible story featuring a series of great hardships). During this time, I worked Job 1 (running my company), Job 2 (real estate agent), and Job 3 (adjunct professor)—plus Mommy. This valley, this low point, was just the final moment of clearing ugly debris from the cotton boll. This scarcity led to clarity. My new focus was ensuring my life would be about resilience—and while this combing process was stretching me to the breaking point, I was not going to break. Plus, through this process, it became clear who was a foe, a frenemy, family, or a true friend. As for true friends, I needed to pay my attorney to keep going on the case—and had run out of money. Three of my dear friends came to the rescue immediately and wired money directly to the lawyer's office, with an open-ended repayment date. Thank you, Cheryl, Tracy, and Pam!

One of the things I ask others when they ask me how I became successful is this: "We all have the same twenty-four hours—what are you doing with yours?"

On the frenemy side of things: In 2011, I had been cast on a show and brought in by a realty team to stage a high-end penthouse, and in 2012, I was flown to a set for an audition. So it felt like TV was a strong possibility—until, shortly after the divorce in 2015, I met with executives from the same design lifestyle TV channel. These executives had an interest in putting me on my own show or in a regular role as part of an ensemble cast. The meetings were going well until one executive said, "Robin sounds too educated. She needs to be more relatable—like more *ghetto fabulous*!"

The room stood still. Heads swiveled in my direction as my jaw dropped. I looked incredulously at that person.

I probably should have stayed quiet, but I said, "You want me to be a stereotype? Not going to do that. I am an educated woman. I am an expert, and you are asking me to sound ghetto fabulous? What does that even mean? You should have a show that shows an educated person in the design world. With my master's degree in real estate finance, we could have a show that breaks down the real costs of purchasing, renovation, and also uses computer models to show how to change a space. It would use technology and make blueprints come alive."

Needless to say, my bluntness, candor, and reaction must have put me on the blacklist because no offer ever materialized from that TV channel. And to this day, I have never been invited back. Should I have handled it differently? Should I have played a stereotype and not myself? Some people would do anything to be on a show, but then they are trapping themselves into a facade that might close doors in the future.

Today, I want to believe it would have been handled differently by decision-makers in that room. Someone should have spoken up and pulled aside that particular executive on the spot to correct their stereotypical comments. Years later, I learned that the same producer and her PR friend started a rumor that I was difficult to work with to cover up their racist commentary, and that hindered my ability to ever get a show under consideration in the very insular lifestyle TV world. Oh well!

My goal has always been authenticity—staying on-brand as an expert, author, and person who is able to do high-level projects that appear in magazines, not a caricature or stereotype.

Pivoting back to real estate: In this industry, you are taught to select intrinsic qualities over superficial ones. For example, you want to make sure the foundation, plumbing, and electrical systems are good. The renovation of a space can be done if the fundamental structure is good, but you may wish to avoid a place with poor structure. Similarly, one should carefully review their criteria for a life partner.

The right intrinsic/structural qualities should be your focus, instead of superficial qualities. Your choice of a partner can profoundly affect your life. Examples of items in a superficial checklist are:

- ☐ Looks: height, hair color, eye color, or weight
- ☐ Education: must be Ivy League, must have a graduate degree, or attend a certain school

- ☐ Job: preferring a certain income level or a white-collar job (Note: Electricians/plumbers/contractors can earn more than some attorneys.)

My dad also said you should know these answers to this intrinsic checklist:

- ☐ Is he kind to waiters? Bus drivers? Janitors? Or to those who can do nothing for him?
- ☐ Is he open to sharing information like where he will be? Or is it one-sided?
- ☐ What is his view of gender roles? Is he a protector, provider, partner, champion?
- ☐ Does he respect his mother? Does he ever refer to women with derogatory names?
- ☐ Does he keep his clothing clean and mended?
- ☐ Does he go to the doctor or dentist or barber?
- ☐ Does he stack up dirty garments for weeks in a hamper instead of washing?
- ☐ Are his shoes polished, and is he "down at the heels" by not keeping his shoes repaired?

A person in their late forties is who they are, and you should accept them as they are. But they should also know that if they want a professional partner, they should expect uncomfortable moments, questions, and reactions, and only with communication and responding will they have an honest relationship.

Sometimes people are not ready because they have not done the work on themselves and are not willing to do the work. Your job is not to fix them. Sometimes walking away may be the best plan.

Before my dad passed, he told me that the truth of a successful relationship is to have these basic questions answered. In his obituary, we added these golden rules for men:

- Never raise a hand to a woman.
- Tell your kids they can always come home.
- Tell your family you love them.
- Polish your shoes.
- Date your wife.
- Show up on time and be present.
- Keep your promises.
- Life is easier if the small things are done with a blessed attitude.

My parents were together for fifty-two years—and it was lovely to see two people who cared about each other and found ways to have fun, vacation together, and disagree respectfully with communication. Both of my parents said: Marriage is an ecosystem. The objective should be that both parties give to each other, acknowledging that sometimes one might need a bit more help (like after pregnancy or a surgery), but overall, it should balance out. And if one person wants it a bit warmer or to keep a window closed during a "nesting time," the other should willingly oblige to minimize stress for the other person.

When you speak to elderly people who still love each other, they speak of the joy they get from giving to their partner and all the experiences they have had together, and they always talk about having their own interests, friends, and hobbies. They are two individuals who make a union with kindness and communication, and not interrogation.

Weaving cotton strands into beautiful fabric requires patience, machinery, and skill, similar to putting one's life back together.

Less than two years after fleeing, I bought the worst house in the best neighborhood. I found it on Craigslist. The owner was penny-wise and pound-foolish by trying to be his own real estate agent, so I got it for far less than the estimated costs. Lesson learned: Things show up when they are meant to, and the only reason I saw this house as a FSBO was because I was looking for a kiddie bicycle, not a house!

At the time, I learned how important relationships are—as one of the artists from the gallery show that was created when I first moved back to New York, Pat Goodman, called me and became a very wise friend who kept reminding me to empower myself. When I moved to my new home, she said, "This is your home, your keys, your locks. You don't have to let anyone into your home unless you want them to be there. And you do not need to follow anyone ever again to try to make a home. You are home."

Her words and kind actions marked the beginning of an awareness that I would never again follow anyone into their life. I truly appreciate her for all her generosity and kindness because she went through a similar situation in her first marriage, and she emerged triumphant in her next life chapter with her second husband. I celebrate her artwork and champion her as a leading force for women's empowerment. One day, she told me that I needed to "remember who I was" and ask myself what "Robin Wilson" would do, and to listen to my own voice, instead of asking others what to do. *Read that sentence again, and put your name in that sentence.*

Through hard work, fortitude, and the regular piecing together of the quilt of life—through weaving and knitting our experiences, wisdom from friends, and penny-pinching—my daughter and I have our own life, identity, home, and a renewed sense of self. It remains important that I honor and reflect on the hard work of my ancestors who believed in my potential, even if they never had a chance to meet me.

QUESTIONS TO COMB THROUGH

1. Have you ever considered divorce but stayed because you thought it was good for the children? Have you considered that negative energy can be more toxic than separating?
2. Can you identify your family, friends, frenemies, and foes? How do you treat your own opinion when you are working through things—do you listen to your inner voice?
3. What are the intrinsic and superficial qualities that you look for in your potential partner before you fall in love? Do you know the difference?

Chapter 13

FINISHING

Raw fabric goes through various steps to enhance its appearance, softness, and durability. These processes include desizing, bleaching, scouring, mercerizing, and singeing. Mercerized fabric is treated with a caustic soda solution to permanently improve its luster, strength, and durability.

Scoured fabric undergoes a chemical cleaning process that removes natural waxes and impurities. After these processes are completed, the fabric is printed and dyed to achieve the desired color and reviewed for feel, strength, luster, and dye affinity. Singed fabric passes quickly over a flame to burn off stray fibers, creating a smoother surface.

Each evening, a colony of bats flies out from under the Congress Avenue Bridge in Austin to the cotton fields out east to feast on insects. They are cleaning the plants so the weevils and other insects do not impede the growth of the cotton plants. Thousands of people show up to watch this spectacle of nature.

Even Whole Foods helps this ecosystem by removing tons of bat guano from under the bridge to be used in gardens around the Austin area, thus protecting the fragile ecosystem. Without the removal of the guano, the bats might move away due to fetid conditions, and fish might die because the water could become too toxic.

An ecosystem is part of the finishing process of life. Every ecosystem goes through a process of starting an action, finishing the action, and repeating to remain viable.

Have you thought of your family and friends as an ecosystem? You start communicating. Positive life moments or challenging situations occur, empathy or wisdom is shared, and issues are resolved—and repeat. Sometimes the frequency of seeing each other will ebb and flow, but your underlying trust and respect will always be there when you see them again.

By 2019, I was ready to quit. Sales had gone sideways after being pulled out of retail, and the cabinetry licensing deal concluded after the kitchen factory was sold. It felt like almost twenty years of hard work had gone down the drain. No pension, no savings, no legacy would be left for my daughter.

In 1999, the windfall from the IPO had allowed me to chase my dream—and in 2019, I was preparing my résumé to start interviewing for a pivot back to a corporate job. I felt shame, sadness, and sheer exhaustion.

At the time, my mom was getting ready to return home to Texas. She was making fewer regular trips to New Jersey so she could continue her caregiver role with Dad, who had multiple health issues. He was a valiant fighter, but his health was fragile. My daughter was in school—in second grade—so I could be a bit more flexible, even if she had to attend an aftercare program at school when I got a job.

I got a few interviews, but every interview turned into a series of questions: "Why do you want a job? We googled you. You should be on our board!" One executive peppered me with questions about how their brand was perceived and ideas I might have to fix certain things, and then he ended the interview with these words: "Thanks for the great advice. I think you are great, but I could never hire you. You would get my job."

But I really needed a job, and I could not be a real estate agent any longer. Although each person in the Sotheby's office was absolutely amazing and professional, it is really tough to go into empty homes with strangers at all hours, put miles on your car when you drive to multiple locations, and then have a buyer come back to the first space, ignore your advice, and underbid—only to have the entire process begin again. Or to have a deal fall through due to financing or inspection issues. All these hours resulted in not getting paid—so a more regular gig was what I was looking for.

I was ready to give up on my two-decade dream that I had worked so hard for. I thought that it was finished, but the universe had other plans . . .

In March 2020, my daughter and her classmates were sent home with a packet of books and homework because a "flu" was going around the school. As a precaution, the parents were told that they would be off campus for a few days. By mid-March, the entire world began to shut down due to the COVID pandemic, and my job search plans ended because we opened school in our home, and I was the teacher.

The silver lining is that within a few days, my book *Clean Design: Wellness for Your Lifestyle*, with its simple tips and tricks for wellness, began to sell again. A few weeks later, we made a "Black Businesses to Support" list, with sales topping $30,000 on one particular day! My job search was officially finished.

We always hear that it is darkest before the dawn, and it is true. So many people would have given up the week or months prior, and taken any job, but that meant that I would not have been able to ship all those orders. Or be a teacher for my daughter. Within weeks, my bank account was made whole and then some. We even started to get work from hoteliers who ordered in semitruck quantities!

During this time, we fully rebranded from an eponymous brand to Clean Design Home®, trademarked it, artmarked the logo so that others could not copy our design, and did a new website. My eponymous brand was finished and served its purpose to make me believe that I could succeed as a brand. Now it was time to set the company on a new path, without using my name so that the firm would be ready for global growth, investors, and a possible exit strategy.

This new beginning was done in stealth mode—with no announcements, just quiet work and a focused strategy to amplify my work on wellness and allergen-aware (or hypoallergenic) products. The timeline for 2020 was intense:

- March: COVID homeschooling begins
- April: New celebrity interior design client
- May: New brand mentioned in magazines, causing a 3,000 percent sales jump overnight
- June: Hospitality orders begin
- July: Trademark/artmark are approved; rebranding underway
- August: New brand licensed to a global manufacturing partner
- September: Market week for the brand launch
- October: Licensing deal signed and then I had to "get to work" to design a collection for the spring market! If the buyers liked the collection, we had a chance to launch in a retail store.
- November: *Inc.* magazine names me to the Top 100 Female Founders list
- December: Segment airs for *The Ellen DeGeneres Show*'s "12 Days of Giveaways"

In 2020, my brand Clean Design Home® was licensed by a company named WestPoint Home. This 250-year-plus legacy textile company had predecessor companies (J. P. Stevens & Co. and Pepperell Manufacturing Company), which operated during the slavery era, when my ancestor Polly arrived in this country, and around the time my family was turning "brown."

The company built great wealth as a northern textile

manufacturer, utilizing its original profits from the use of raw materials (cotton) planted, picked, and processed with enslaved labor until sharecropping took hold after emancipation.

The irony of being selected to join their roster of brands in 2020 was an opportunity to highlight our country's progress. At the time, we had built a twenty-year history as a lifestyle brand for wellness-oriented and allergen-aware consumers. In spring 2021, the brand was presented during the Spring Market in New York. It was exciting to see the brand picked up by retail buyers and officially slated to land in Macy's flagship store for the 2021 holiday season. Over time, we saw the brand added to many other retailers and positioned globally with military outpost stores.

By the end of 2021, our new pop-up retail section in Macy's was a fiscal success. Having been an alumnus of the Workshop at Macy's program a decade earlier, this was a dream come true! It was as if the foundation had been laid a decade earlier, before ending the "business is my boyfriend" phase. This moment was perfect timing!

In 2024, I realized that it was time to open a retail store of our own to protect the brand and create a marketing opportunity. I tried to strategically communicate with our licensing partner and learned that sometimes it is better to "buy back your license" and not to renew a contract if your vision is not aligned.

Some momentum we had as a brand upon entering the licensing deal was eventually lost due to staff changes. And I realized that it was time to "buy back" (not renew) the license upon its expiration. I learned a lesson and decided to "never allow someone else to control the brand narrative" unless we were in full alignment as partner and firm.

Full circle . . . combing the cotton and finishing a lap . . . remembering who I was before . . . and on a bigger stage. By September 2025, with an economic slump at retailers due to global tariffs, we decided not to sign an offered licensee extension. In the parlance of the industry, "we bought our license back"—and our freedom.

At some point, someone tallied up my brand's cumulative licensed brand revenue—it topped $100 million—revenue we have helped other companies make, while receiving only a small percentage. The wildest irony is that all these years, I have approached organizations to get funding to grow, with commentary during the pitches that there is proof of concept, a track record, a founder who pulled herself up by her bootstraps, and all the other keywords that seem to work for others. And after twenty-five years of hard work, my firm has never received significant outside funding—in fact, my home has sometimes been my bank—utilizing funds that should have paid a mortgage to pay my team and teetering on the edge of foreclosure at least four times! I read Kevin M. Polston's biography on Byron Allen and feel sometimes that if Allen's success is any indication, it is darkest before the dawn, because he has really crushed it as an entrepreneur with his media company, and he writes about using his home as his bank too—with limited funding options!

The most important lesson is that you must always remain firmly in control of your brand and be the steward of your vision. There may be others who think that they can "interpret" the designs, and they may have great talents in that area, but at the end of the day, it is your vision and your brand. You get the final sign-off. Your directness may rub a staff member or a partner the wrong way, but they are in a role to assist you—and to work as a partner on behalf of the brand.

> The universe would not have let you come this far if you were not meant to have this opportunity.

You are the brand. Your company has your name or brand on the door. You have to start over if it does not work out, and that individual who is creating barriers will likely get another paycheck or a new job easily.

You are one-of-one. It is hard to redefine yourself when you have lived more than twenty-five years as a brand. What "job" can you do? You need to believe you have earned and deserve your seat at the table.

The lessons I learned from building a brand are:

- Think of your brand as a luxury vehicle. Give the valet key to the parking team, but keep your house keys and main key fob on your person. Do not give the entire key ring to someone else, and make sure they keep their hands firmly on the wheel until they really know how to drive your vehicle.
- If someone tells you to stop sharing your successes or telling others about your brand or company, you should

know that they are either a frenemy or foe. Because just like the religious Sunday school song, "This little light of mine / I'm gonna let it shine . . . hide it under a bushel, NO! / I'm gonna let it shine . . ."

- Always have people around you who will act in the best interest of your brand that you have worked so hard to build. If you discover that they are not partners, walk away.
- Ensure that you vocalize your opinions, even if others disagree. Collaborate and hear the "why," and if an employee starts to create a negative corporate culture or they tear you down behind your back, let them find an opportunity that will make them happy, just not in your realm.
- It is your responsibility to protect your brand and your team when you are the leader.
- Jealousy and negative energy always come from those who are watching on the sidelines as critics—and those who want to ascend with you or who are ahead of you are often ready and willing to help. Stick with those who have already made it up the mountain.

Our retail store venture at an NYC-area mall closed after six months. I heard through the grapevine that a frenemy said, "She failed." What she did not realize was that the pop-up store actually succeeded. It was a marketing vehicle to build brand awareness. We gained thousands of local customers, we have their contact information, and they are comfortable buying online because they "experienced" the products in person and know our quality. With increased brand recognition, we tripled our online sales and direct-to-consumer business. We also learned some lessons that we can take forward should we decide to do another pop-up.

> Taking a risk means you tried.
> Talk means nothing.
> Action is a fact.

Always remember that there are a lot of critics on the sidelines who would never have the courage to take the risk. But an entrepreneur gets up every day—often paying others and not themselves—to chase a dream. And then they do it the next day, week, month, year . . .

In early 2025, I appeared on-air for HSN twice. As we watched the sales numbers, it was clear that economic issues were affecting so many consumers, and we had a sheet set that was priced right for the consumer. There may be economic challenges, but always remember that when there is a downturn in the economy and you find your niche, it is a moment when everything is possible. For example, with the right marketing, Kellogg's sold cereal with a toy inside during the Depression—and their competitor, Post, simply kept their pricing. Because they took advantage of the affordability niche, at a time when parents during the Depression had to choose between toys and food, and they provided both, Kellogg's gained market dominance for over fifty years.

Just like fabric is singed with a pass over an open flame to burn off stray fibers, my firm has done the same with our business: reviewing all partners, personnel, and product placement to ensure fiscal responsibility. Lesson learned: No one will ever care for your brand or legacy as much as you do. Resistance to your vision will always require that you make tough choices that may involve scouring, singeing, or scraping—just like you have to do to finish a fabric, as you move to the final stage of the cotton journey!

Questions to Comb Through

1. Have you had a moment in your professional life where the act of scouring or singeing your inner circle might remove barriers to your next level of growth or success?
2. Do you believe in coincidence, or do you recognize that a vision board is actually telling the universe and you where you want to go?
3. Do you have anyone in your inner circle (including your spouse or partner) who acts like your big moments are little? Do they have any jealousy over your success?

Chapter 14

CONSTRUCTION

Finished fabrics are inspected for flaws and then cut and sewn into finished products. When you compare your life to the construction of a custom-made garment, it mirrors the unique, layered, and transformative journey of life. A garment begins with the original product: cotton. Then a muslin prototype is adjusted, broken apart, and fitted until the best shape is created. The finished product is constructed with invisible scaffolds—hand stitching, linings, and draping—until it is perfect: a beautiful exterior that is only capable of holding its shape because of the painstaking work and resilience to construct unseen layers beneath.

Constructing a new life, new career, new home, or new brand requires one word: resilience.

As mentioned throughout this book, every chapter required some form of construction, and in this last chapter, it has been clear that for the past few months, my business, brand, and life have been under reconstruction. The brand has decoupled from a textile license, and we are refocused on working with new manufacturers. Our focus is establishing global partnerships and legacy building, all while managing through tariffs and a global economic rebalancing.

Recently, I was asked this question at an event: "How did you rise to a new, higher level when everything crumbled?"

My response is, "Resilience is the answer. The moment I stopped being the character in the story and became the chairman of the board for my life, everything changed. I literally took a giant piece of paper and combed through the following: decisions made on my life journey, missteps and mistakes, skills assessments, connections, brand goals, personal goals, and more. The first column was: What do I have? And the next column: What do I want? And finally: What or who can help bridge that gap?"

Resilience requires you to acknowledge the messy parts and find a process that is intentional and transformative as you work on reconstruction.

I believe that my childhood with chores, an allowance, and adults who listened and believed in me was the strongest gift and the generational-wealth foundation for my success.

Have you ever thought about treating the construction of your life like an engineering project? Ask yourself about the structure and your foundation, windows, walls, ceilings, interior, and doors.

Imagine the square house with a triangle on top that most children draw. Think of the four corners as daily survival, short-term goals, details, and a regular income stream. The roof is the long-term vision, and each corner of the square is needed to support the triangular roof.

When you look at your scaffolding with those questions, you realize the discipline required to analyze each of these goals with cold, hard logic. This is one of the most powerful acts of kindness you can perform for Brand You. It is the antithesis of defeat or despair—it is empowerment and the basis for resilience.

At the end of this scaffolding process, you will have built a blueprint—a plan of action and mandate. Resilience is all about figuring out what you need to do to move forward, not waiting for the phone to ring. But if it does ring, answer it and return the call!

Clearly review your options to prioritize your next move. Make the strategic moves that matter the most.

My soundtrack during one rebuilding moment included Jill Scott's "Golden," Aretha Franklin's "Respect," Alicia Keys's "Superwoman," Nina Simone's "Feeling Good" and "Sinnerman," Miley Cyrus's "The Climb" and "Flowers," Beyoncé's "Run the World (Girls)," and Nat King Cole's version of "Who's Sorry Now?"

From seedling to the cotton gin to the finished fabric—metaphorically, I went to the bottom of the sea and had to climb mountains and then soar like a phoenix—a robin flying like an eagle!

Resilience meant understanding that the disconnect between my public profile and the reality of my finances was huge, and thus, my life remains literally under construction.

Let's go back to the moment when I sat in the living room of my new home. I was broke and trying to figure out the next step, and I knew that there was limited time to craft a plan.

"Mom, I am going to go toward the light, not the darkness," I said.

She shook her head. "You may feel despair, and you may feel like this rough time defines you, but the reality is that this test is one you must pass for the universe to let you go to the next level."

On the phone later that day, a childhood friend said, "Robin, you are like a phoenix—you will rise, and you will be a great example to your daughter and other women. You should not be afraid to speak about your domestic violence experience because you now have a platform. Too many people are silent. Seeing things with your own eyes makes you know that those struggles are real."

Both of them asked me, "What is your plan? We know that you have fought a relentless battle—you had to pay lawyers all your money. What are you going to do?"

I replied, "I have about $200 in my bank account, and all my money is going to legal bills. I am going to rebuild. But every time I try to get a job, I get rejected because my public image makes them question why a successful entrepreneur would want to be working for them instead of being on their board. So, I have to bet on myself now."

My childhood friend said, "Maybe it is time to use your graduate degree and get your real estate license, learn the craft, and pay off the legal bills. You may even meet a developer that you can partner with—and you will be able to work hours around school."

So what did I do? I used my last $200 to pay for the real estate coursework, finished in a week, got sponsored by a leading agency to hold my license, and started to reconstruct my life with a plan for three years, and it worked! *Seedlings grow roots that create plants.*

And then what? I became a master juggler. Ignoring fear and focusing solely on "my business being my boyfriend" again propelled me further and faster than before. In order to propel your business to the next level, you must let go of certain things (or else you will be stretched) and move forward with clarity. This requires a strategy and focused execution with a one-step-at-a-time approach, instead of a desperate jump. Always create the strategy first so that you can reach a goal.

Just as financial pressure was peaking and the weight of trying to reconstruct my life felt almost too heavy to bear, something extraordinary happened. In 2019, a person walking by the real estate office (Job 2) saw my photo, called, and gave me a listing for a $2 million property. It sold during the first showing for all cash. It was unexpected and landed in my lap. The high commission provided an instant, substantial financial safety net. In classical literature, those moments are called deus ex machina (god out of the machine), and it was a miraculous solution to what felt like an impossible problem. *Always express gratitude!*

The moment that real estate listing came in, I chuckled and looked skyward—and my real estate agent career was complete.

It was perfectly timed and paid off the last of my legal bills. It felt like the universe was saying, "We see you. We see the work you are doing. And we are glad you did not quit, because we have a bigger plan." In 2020, we all know what exciting moments happened for my brand. *It is always darkest before the dawn.*

Spring break 2021 was the dawn (or so I thought!)—my mom had returned home, my finances were more stable, and my daughter and I were going to Texas for a visit! My daughter was now eight years old, and the last time she had seen her grandfather had been only a few years earlier, but children from ages six to eight need more time in person with a grandparent to build a stronger memory, even with regular video chats.

Dad only had 20 percent hearing in one ear—a side effect from a glioblastoma brain surgery (from which he lived longer than expected). To allow conversation in our video calls, I had downloaded a software where we could speak, and Dad could read the words on the screen. One day, my daughter was on the video call showing him some of her artwork, and she just said, "I love you, Grandpa." When the transcribed words crossed the screen, my dad began to show his emotions and started to brush away tears. My mom just hugged him. My daughter asked, "Are you okay, Grandpa?" My dad just chuckled and said, "Yes, baby. I love you too! I think that there is some dust in the air." And then he just smiled at her.

The world was in the middle of the COVID-19 pandemic. I scheduled a trip to Texas, but my mom wanted us to wait until this pandemic was over, especially because she was afraid that we would infect Dad, who was in frail health. Everything in my being decided that waiting was not a good idea, especially as she kept indicating that he was not doing well. So we flew to Austin, wearing surgical masks on the plane. When we landed, Mom picked us up, and we drove straight to Costco and decided that we would create a "pod" with meals at home to protect Dad. When we arrived at the house, my daughter ran toward my dad, and he picked her up and swung her around. Both of them just reconnected instantly—grandfather and grandchild. Mom and I stood off to the side and beamed, taking photos of them as they walked the property and found a bunny, opossum, and a fire ant trail near the old wagon wheel. I think that I got a hug a few hours later.

We had only two outings around a lot of people: the Kalahari water park and go-karts at the Circuit of the Americas track. Everything else was outdoors if we met with relatives or friends—including a tennis moment, where Dad and his only living brother could watch my daughter play. She is such a good tennis player and my dad, mom, and uncle cheered from the sidelines!

The entire spring break was perfect weather, and my daughter and dad just bonded. They played checkers, they walked together to the mailbox every day, and they laughed and talked with his hearing aid on maximum or the software on-screen translating her words. Mom and I just watched with joy as we worked to prepare the next meal. I also slept, as this was one of the first times since the divorce where my parents were in charge as grandparents. My daughter had so much fun walking around the land, feeding the chickens and goats, and petting the sheep at the house of a neighbor, and then driving down the road to see the longhorn cattle. My city kid was thrilled to see wildlife and country animals that were not in a petting zoo.

As our trip came to a close, I felt that this might be the last time I would see my dad alive. He was frail, and as we were about to go to the airport, I asked Mom to stop the car. I ran back into the house and hugged him tight. We both looked into each other's eyes, and he just said, "Robin, I love you. You take care of my grandbaby, and you have made me so proud. I know it has been hard the past few years, but you made the right decision to leave. Your little girl is so wonderful. I believe she will do great things too. I love you." And with that, I held his hand with interlocked fingers and held back the tears as I left the side of his recliner so we could make it to the airport.

My daughter turned nine in September and returned to the classroom while the pandemic continued to rage. And then Mom called in October and said Dad had caught COVID and was hospitalized. His health declined rapidly, and in November, he passed. Mom and Dad had been married fifty-two years, and she described the moment she walked out of the hospital with his wallet and personal possessions—but not him. She called me from the car, but I had left my phone in the house as I walked my daughter to school. When I got back in the house, there were messages waiting. The phone rang again. Time stopped. Tears flowed. An eerie feeling of loss. And now as the only living child, I knew that I should be there to help my mom with arrangements.

Dad died on a Monday. Just days later, on Thursday, my former spouse took me to court saying that he objected to my daughter going to the funeral of her grandfather and missing school for a few days, even though the school was fine with her remote learning. Can you imagine, in the middle of processing the loss of your father, getting multiple emails, shedding tears of grief, and getting served court papers?

And on Friday, only four days after the death of my father, I had to appear in front of a judge in tears to defend my travel to Texas and why, as the only child, I needed to go home to help my mom plan the funeral. The judge granted travel but with a few days' delay, so I was unable to be present to help my mother with arrangements, and my daughter and I almost missed the wake due to the travel delays. Domestic violence continues to occur after you flee!

Grieving while fighting a court battle. My father's funeral delayed until the following weekend due to a former spouse. Be careful who you marry, as emotional abuse and gaslighting will continue even after a divorce.

Grief comes in waves, and there were moments when I felt guilty because my mom spent so much time helping me during the post-divorce era. She told me that she and Dad had been 100 percent behind me and that while my dad had held certain opinions when he met my ex-husband, he kept them to himself.

He was always thrilled to have a grandchild and legacy to continue the family progress. I missed some of the last years of his life, mired in the post-divorce drama that led to a lifetime final restraining order against my former spouse. My dad was clear: Fifty-two years of marriage meant that he and Mom experienced ups and downs, ins and outs—but at the end of the day, even if there were times when both of them did not "like" each other, they always loved each other and respected each other—and he *never* put his hands on my mother.

He believed in a man's role to protect, and if Mom would be happier going to a market five miles down the road, that is the market that we went to. Dad was very happy that my daughter and I had created a new "home" and that his daughter was safe.

> A family tree can wither when no one
> tends to its roots.
> The potential for greatness lies within each of us
> and we must celebrate our history.
> What legacy will you leave?

Several colleagues, clients, and students have asked me for a few words of wisdom about the entrepreneurial mindset. I have created a list to share about the stages you may experience as you transition through life. Here are some insights:

Metamorphosis: Like a butterfly, we sometimes must deliberately shed the past to make room for the future. A move to a new home, a revision of our wardrobe, a new haircut, a new relationship. A simple process that requires you to leave behind the old version of yourself for the next to emerge. Shed that cocoon and let the beautiful wings emerge! Similarly, you can put a coat of paint on a crumbling house with a poor interior—but things will start to break again quickly. But if you tear it down from the inside out and rebuild it, that house will stand for decades. *Resilience requires total transformation.*

Foundation: My great-grandfather focused on one question: Did you respect your parents? Both my grandfathers focused on work ethic and shared legacy knowledge about organic food (paternal) and entrepreneurship (maternal). Both grandmothers showered me with love and lessons about keeping a home, spirituality, and comportment. My parents focused on education. *Core family values and education have been the foundation of my American Dream.*

Windows: Imagine me in third grade with metal braces on my legs and plaster molds in my orthopedic shoes. A few years later, a model scout sees me and views my look as having unlimited potential. I did the work with my diet, practiced my posture, and pranced while watching and mimicking the CNN fashion program—which prepared me to construct my new identity as pretty Robin instead of nerdy, bullied Robin. This required an identity transplant and a focus on unique positive attributes. *Feel worthy enough to be in the room, not just peeking through the window.*

Ceilings and Walls: In order to survive the Jim Crow world, my great-grandfather passed when he needed to do business in Houston. There were invisible rules with very visible signs in spaces where he was not welcome if they knew he was a person of color. But he did not choose to live by those rules—he made his own way and did not let a chorus of "No" or "Not welcome" limit his view of possibility.

Throughout history, there have been mavericks who challenged the system, realizing that the key to not internalizing a disappointment is to realize that the "No" is not about your capability. It may simply mean you need to do a bit more analysis. Ask yourself: "How do I bridge this gap? How do I make my goals a reality?" *Treat each closed door as a data point.*

Kick yourself off the bottom of a valley, hill, or mountain, and then choose where you surface. The height to which you ascend can be blocked by a chorus of "No" moments or a series of "Maybe" instances, but rarely will you get an easy street filled with "Yes" responses. Each time you hear rejection, you must remember that it is not a brick wall or ceiling—but a chance to do a pivot, which may require you to revise your looks, résumé, pitch deck, or presentation. *It is about resilience.*

Interiors: This is the story of my home purchase. The bones of the house were good—the heating, electrical, plumbing—but the interior was definitely not ready for photography. But what was more important in the long term—structure or cosmetics?

At this moment, ask yourself what your internals look like. Are you focused on wellness for yourself so that you have more time to complete your journey? Have you created a methodical plan that relies on more than grit and hope? Have you created a vision board (ideas), grid chart (plan), or timeline that gives you an honest assessment of assets, connections, and measurable steps needed to get from Point A to Point B? *Create a vision board for your dreams.*

Doors: When a point of entry is blocked due to reasons unknown—gender, experience, pitch deck, etc.—you must find a locksmith (e.g., a coach, mentor, or master class) to guide you on how to open it. The other option is to remain sullenly on the lawn having a pity party! *Find your mentor or sponsor.*

Transformation: When I look at this moment in my business, we have walked away from certain partnerships, stopped certain ways of doing business, and canceled certain ways of thinking. To that end, using technology, the business transformation is real, tangible, and nonnegotiable—for example:

- Extensive travel has changed with technology, and with video meetings, I am more efficient and actually able to do more self-care and spend more time building my business with flexibility at home instead of traveling and spend fewer days in the office.

- Our rebranding in 2020 from an eponymous name to an exit strategy name transitioned our thinking from "Robin is the brand" to "Clean Design is a protocol, and our Clean Design Home® brand has products for the community that provide a solution." It changed from a person to being part of a massive ecosystem brand focused on wellness.
- Our original goal was to be in stores, but we have seen a trend that online sales offer greater ROI versus in-person retail placement. In fact, the chargebacks from retail stores can be more than actual sales due to customer mishandling of merchandise—e.g., you cannot sell a dirty pillow or sheets. After someone opens the package or steps on the items in the aisle, it will be returned to the merchant, resulting in a loss of revenue.
- Pop-up shops are mostly effective as a marketing tool and a way for a brand to understand regional demographics.

We started this book with ancestry and history, and we end it with destiny and legacy. Failure has occupied a few moments, but only because a risk was taken. Find a niche that will help people, stay on your path, and always remember to keep your hand on the wheel of your brand. While you must delegate to grow the brand, make sure that if someone has shown no results within four to six months, you put your hand back on the wheel and let them go, especially if they cannot articulate their strategy.

Never feel that you must keep someone on your team, *especially as a small business entrepreneur*, because their salary could be funds that you could be paying yourself. You should not feel guilty about letting go of someone who is argumentative, negative, or not pushing the ball up the hill for your company or brand. If they are not performing, you are simply paying them to keep a seat warm. The greatest gift you can give them, and yourself, is to do weekly check-ins, especially if people are working remotely.

I recently taught graduate-level students in a capsule course called "The Entrepreneurial Mindset." The textbook selected was *The E-Myth* by Michael Gerber, and the general premise of the book is that you should write a job description for every role you perform as your business starts. Then, you should fire yourself from certain roles as your business grows. Never say "I'll do it myself"—instead, make your team accountable for performing their role. In other words: Fire yourself from a job when you hire someone! The following list will share some experiences that I have had as an entrepreneur. Until I "fired myself" from certain roles, there was no accountability, and we did not progress. When you build a team with clarity, you can see who is just getting a paycheck, and who is helping your business grow.

- I hired someone for a sales role, and after paying them a stipend for six months, there were zero sales and a lot of "pipeline" talk. When they were let go, we did not get one return phone call or email from their contacts, which means there was no pipeline.

- Another time, someone was hired for marketing and events, and they quit on the same day that they were going to be fired. We also learned that for a launch event to be held in two weeks, no venue had been booked, and no invitations had been prepared. We still had a great event, and the funny thing is, the person who did not do their job proceeded to make childish negative posts on social media. But the truth is that they used what we paid them to pay for an event they were hosting—and they made our event (their job!) secondary.
- We hired a social media person who made us pay for a dashboard and a monthly retainer, and told us that our engagement had increased. By the time they were terminated nine months later, our following had gone down by thousands of people due to erratic posting and imagery that was not uplifting. Within weeks of this termination, we started making regular posts and engaging with influencers ourselves. We gained three thousand new followers on Instagram within three months.

These examples are to remind you of the metaphor that you must be the pilot of your helicopter—and touch down when you need to review the work of your team. But always stay at the macro level to ensure that your vision is realized.

Remind yourself of the many steps for cotton: From seeds to growth to the harvest process, there is so much combing to remove debris. Stretch fibers as far as possible, until finally you have a finished product that is ready for the beautiful fabrics we see everywhere.

From the field to the factory to the fabrication—cotton only reaches its potential after being combed, tested, and remaining resilient.

Combing cotton is a metaphor for the process we can all employ in our lives to be our best selves. **I believe that Brand You is worth it!**

QUESTIONS TO COMB THROUGH

1. Exterior looks may hide the interior work needed to sustain you and your home. Have you decided to work on the cosmetic or the structural?
2. Do you need to honor your resilience and how you have persisted even when things were challenging?
3. Have you ever touched a cotton boll to see how it feels on the exterior and interior? Can you imagine how far it is from the origin of the cotton fibers to creating the finest garments or linens?

Epilogue

Dear Reader,

I got this book deal in January 2025, and two months later, I was at the doctor's office when a routine checkup required a mammogram, then a callback, and then a fearful conversation with an oncologist, followed by a lumpectomy surgery—and then waiting for results. After a few days of fear and then getting the call from the surgeon that the tissue was benign, I finally exhaled and looked into the eyes of my child, and both of us cheered, and our tension was finally released. But I still have to be vigilant every few months for the next few years.

I am now even more focused on wellness: rest, diet, and stress management. And toxic people and their energy remain at arm's length. Certain people said words, but just like Pooh said, "You know it . . ."

Recently, I watched *The Secret* again and listened to podcasts from Brené Brown and Mel Robbins and have been able to speak with the amazing Linda Clemons!

A few friends recognized that I had been stuck, and they reminded me who I was as a person, not as a brand. Those talks were so therapeutic and kind. I remain so grateful for the ladies who showed up to a catered luncheon one day, with all the kids playing outside. It was a day that I will never forget, and you know who you are.

Each day that I walk this earth, I learn more about people, friends, and family. Some of you may not be as close as we once were, but it is likely because we are all working all the time. I miss you and want to thank you for the role you played in my current chapter, which brings us here—to this book. *Combing Cotton* is all about the steps you take to become your best self!

I have learned that success is not about competition—it is about staying on a trajectory and running your own race. My purpose is to be a good example to my daughter with a strong work ethic and resilience, and to provide a full life for her so that she will metamorphose into a beautiful butterfly.

Betting on me means that I acknowledge the many moments that required resilience, fortitude, and reflection. Thanks to the ancestors who traveled the Middle Passage, were part of the Boston Tea Party, endured slavery and Jim Crow, and paved the way for me to get a good education, my future is brighter due to your strength. Thank you!

As a wise woman said, "Run your race. Stay focused on your lane. Be aware of what other people are doing, but they were put on this earth to complete a different trajectory. You are one-of-one. Stay focused on your big dream and do it well. And each time you pivot, things get really hard. The ones who show grit and determination typically get to the next level—as most people give up." I remind myself daily that:

- Polly did not give up on her journey through the Middle Passage.
- Grandpapa did not give up when his son died after rejection from a nearby hospital; he and Grandmother simply moved out of sharecropping to give my dad a chance in Austin.
- Great Granddaddy passed when he needed to build a business in real estate, own parking lots and a general store, and more to create generational wealth.
- Dad did his own firsts as an Austin city bus driver, as one of the first interstate motorcoach drivers, and joining the Teamsters. In his wry sense of humor, he said, he always knew he had a bathroom at the back of the bus! He drove presidents, movie stars, rock stars, and athletes, and kept them safe!
- Mom has protected me and selflessly given to me all these years, and as of the writing of this book, she visited for Thanksgiving and decorated the Christmas tree with my daughter—and I love the laughter and joy they share. I am so blessed to have had this loving helicopter mom, even though I did not appreciate it when I was younger!
- As a Gold Star family member, I was grateful for the opportunity to meet with the US Army and US Marine Corps to provide a quality bedding option for troops and their families.
- My daughter—she is so gifted in academics and tennis. I wish that my parents had had the money when I was young and that I had had the health to do what she is able to do as an athlete. I love her response to a question

I ask her daily before bed: "Who are you?" She has a ready response: "I am beautiful, smart, funny, kind, and loved." I hope that she teaches her future children the same words because most people forget that it is not what you do, but the qualities you have intrinsically—your character, morals, ethics, and being one-of-one. Take the weaving/knitting learned in your youth and comb out the debris!

To all of you: No matter how hard it feels sometimes, remember that your life is about resilience. Who are you to stop now? Your uniqueness is unmatched and unrivaled. Remember that you are always going to be one-of-one: Brand You!

Much love and gratitude,

Historical Details

Stephen F. Austin—the man—was focused on fulfilling his father's dying wishes to bring cotton to Texas on a major scale. He was one of the early champions who worked hard to establish Texas as the next great cotton frontier of the South. At Austin's invitation, cotton planters began to move westward into Texas from already established Southern states such as Mississippi, Georgia, and Alabama. During the Civil War, even more planters escaped to Texas, moving their enslaved people westward with them.

Enslaved persons who were "lucky" enough to get on the boats destined for the United States were sold like cattle to work on plantations to harvest much of the country's raw materials, including soybeans, tobacco, and cotton. Many used their native agricultural knowledge to contribute to the growth of this nation—with no compensation and often facing cruelty due to the color of their skin.

But their fate was often better than that of those trafficked to other nations. Cotton had been cultivated, spun, and woven into useful materials for generations in Nigeria and Senegal. Enslaved people were trafficked through Senegal and Nigeria as they were currency for war and despotic leaders. They were sold after being kidnapped, chained, and traded. They were then sent across the oceans to various ports, including Brazil, Cuba, the Dominican Republic, Haiti, Guyana, and the United States.

The ancestral journey of my family from forced labor to a strong work ethic required that I comb the cotton to learn more about how much progress this nation and my hardworking family have made in five generations. But we must all continue the work to recognize the legacy of our families who often came to this country with very little—and sharing my family details may open doors, I hope, for future generations!

Cotton continues to be valued for its resilience and adaptability. It is still used for clothing (both utilitarian and fashionable), canvas, rope, paper, currency, and medical supplies. NASA incorporates cotton in clothing worn on the International Space Station. Piezoelectric cotton fabrics produce electricity from movement, used in self-powered wearable electronics. Cotton is used in 3D printing, prototyping biodegradable products, and medical implants. It protects and medicates wounds via controlled drug release. Today, combined with nanoparticles or natural microbial agents, it is used as a self-sterilizing fabric for hospital gowns, masks, and wound dressings. When blended with other high-performance fibers, such as Kevlar, it offers lifesaving, lightweight, flexible body armor to the military and law enforcement.

And, of course, cotton is used in bedding.

Historical Details

I wrote this book because of serendipity—how the collision of our ancestors, our dreams, and reality shapes our lives.

- Imagine being the grandchild of a cotton sharecropper who now has a global brand with products made of cotton. Imagine being the great-grandchild of an entrepreneur who now operates a design-focused business.
- Imagine learning about Eli Whitney and the cotton gin as a schoolgirl—and then, in your early twenties, being invited to spend the night in the Tanglewood area home of a Whitney descendant.
- Imagine attending Stephen F. Austin High School, being elected student council president, and being honored by the Hall of Honor in 2013 while having heard stories from your father about the effects of "separate but equal" while he was in high school at L.C. Anderson High. My dad's school in the 1950s received hand-me-down books from my alma mater with missing pages and epithets on the pages that remained.
- Imagine being at HSN in their Tampa studios in 2025, nearly 600 miles away from the steaming, long-gone wharves of the Port of New Orleans, to film in-studio for your Clean Design Home® bedding line. You then go to a studio where unseen staffers have created two completely furnished bedrooms, set up to display your beautifully designed bedding. You stand by one bed, your fingertips lightly brushing the smooth surface of one duvet cover, being careful not to dent or wrinkle the fabric. Your ancestors could never have imagined this moment, yet they paved the way.

It is impossible to remember Eli Whitney's invention of the cotton gin without also recognizing the technology's contribution to antebellum slavery.

1790. There are six slave states in the United States.

1794. Eli Whitney and Phineas Miller patent the cotton gin—a mere quarter century before Polly, my fourth great-grandmother, arrives in the United States.

1807. Congress abolishes the foreign slave trade, a ban that goes into effect on January 1, 1808. **After this date, importing enslaved people from Africa becomes illegal in the United States.**

1815. Polly is born in Africa.

1819. Polly arrives as human cargo at the Port of New Orleans in 1819. Cotton has become one of the most valuable crops in the United States.

1860. Texas is ranked fifth among Confederate states in cotton production. Its output grows rapidly due to expansive land that is suitable for cotton cultivation, especially in East and Central Texas, with a mild winter climate and long growing season. Consequently, Black enslaved people make up over 30 percent of the population in many of the cotton-producing counties in Texas.

At that time and even today, cotton is valued for its resilience, versatility, absorbency, flexibility, and ability to stand up to environmental stresses while still a plant in the ground of the proverbial plantation. When picked, the cotton bolls are pulled apart, combed multiple times—initially by hand—until twisted into thread, woven into fabric, and finally transformed into currency, clothing, canvas, sails, rope, sack cloth, paper, feed bags, grain sacks, medical supplies (rolled bandages were used fifty years later in the Civil War), tablecloths, and bedding.

All this was a very labor-intensive process **until the invention of the cotton gin, which made slavery more profitable.** Prior to the cotton gin, short-staple cotton had to be picked and cleaned by hand. A cotton gin could remove seeds and debris from cotton more efficiently than a plantation's slave labor.

The cotton gin revolutionized cotton production in the United States—benefiting Southern plantations, Northern textile mills, financial institutions, shipping companies, and multiple other businesses and individuals connected to the institution of slavery. An enslaved person could produce approximately five pounds of lint cotton daily. Whitney's hand-powered cotton gin could produce approximately fifty pounds of lint cotton daily. The steam-powered cotton gins used at the time of the Civil War were producing nearly 2,500 pounds of lint cotton daily.

Cotton became the South's most important crop and the leading US export. Yet the cotton gin also had a significant human cost. Although cotton production became more efficient with the cotton gin, more slave labor was needed to plant and harvest the cotton as the number and size of plantations grew to keep up with demand.

As slave owners benefited from the success of cotton, the lives of the enslaved people they owned were made more challenging. Tobacco farmers who now found less demand for their crop began to sell enslaved people to cotton plantation owners for higher prices. Cotton farmers, who may have considered freeing enslaved people, now found them more valuable as property to be traded. Northern slave owners, who lived in states that were abolishing slavery, chose to sell "property" to Southern masters and split up families for a profit rather than lose money from legal emancipation. The lives of free Blacks in the North were more precarious as they faced the risk of being kidnapped and then sold to Southern plantation owners—with no repercussions—by self-appointed posse members seeking a bounty.

Between the years 1820 and 1860, approximately 80 percent of the global cotton supply was produced in the United States. Nearly all the exported cotton was shipped to Great Britain, fueling its burgeoning textile industry and making the powerful British empire increasingly dependent on American cotton and Southern slavery. New Orleans, the hub of commerce, boasted the largest slave market in the United States and grew to become the nation's fourth-largest city as a result. Slaves, cotton, and the steamship transformed the city from a relatively isolated corner of North America to a thriving metropolis that rivaled New York in importance.

There were fifteen slave states, and more than one-third of the population of the southern portion of the US was enslaved. From 1790 to 1860, the enslaved population grew from roughly 790,000 to 4 million. Annual cotton production grew from 2,000 bales to almost 5 million bales.

Approximately one million enslaved people were sold from northern states and the upper south to the lower south to meet the demand for producing cotton. This process became known as the internal slave trade, or the largest forced migration in American history, leading to the destruction of numerous families.

Historical Details

Cotton and slavery occupied a central—and intertwined—place in the nineteenth-century economy. About 75 percent of the cotton produced in the United States was eventually exported abroad. Exporting at such high volumes made the United States the undisputed world leader in cotton production. Even after the Civil War, cotton was still considered the country's most valuable export.

Cotton planters projected the amount of cotton they could harvest based on the number of enslaved people under their control. In general, planters expected a good "hand," or slave, to work ten acres of land and pick two hundred pounds of cotton a day. An overseer or master measured each slave's daily yield. Great pressure existed to meet the expected daily amount, and some masters whipped enslaved people who picked less than expected.

Cotton harvesting occurred as many as seven times a season as the plant grew and continued to produce bolls through the fall and early winter. During the picking season, enslaved people worked from sunrise to sunset with a ten-minute break at lunch; many slaveholders tended to give them little to eat, since spending on food would cut into their profits.

The South's dependence on cotton was matched by its dependence on enslaved people to harvest cotton. Despite the rhetoric of the American Revolution that "all men are created equal," slavery not only endured in the American republic but formed the very foundation of the country's economic success.

In school, many were taught that Abraham Lincoln freed enslaved people with the Emancipation Proclamation on January 1, 1863. But Texas students were taught that word did not reach Texas until two years later, on June 19, 1865, when the Union General Gordon Granger rode to Galveston and announced General Order Number 3, proclaiming the freedom of enslaved people in the state of Texas, a date which officially marked the end of slavery in the United States.

In 1865, there were more than 430,000 enslaved people in Texas positioned to keep fueling cotton production. Even though slavery had officially disappeared, the people had not, and there was no mechanism to educate or empower all the former enslaved people. Yet there remained a need for humans to cultivate and pick the cotton crop from fields.

Cotton was immensely important to the Texas economy—economically, culturally, and politically. While the Civil War disrupted production, cotton remained the dominant cash crop and the backbone of the state's agricultural system both before and after emancipation.

Enter tenant farming and sharecropping. Even though those two terms are commonly used interchangeably in casual conversation, there are significant differences:

- Tenant farmers (often white) have more economic independence in that they own or rent their equipment and supplies. Tenant farmers have more control over what they plant and where they sell it.
- Sharecroppers own nothing and have little to no decision-making power. The landowner owns everything: land, seed, tools, production, sales, and housing. The sharecroppers officially are paid a share of the crop's

yield. The landowner markets the crop and controls the finances, so the sharecropper is often left in debt.

In short, sharecropping was just another version of slavery, with workers trapped in cycles of debt and dependency on landowners for everything, an ecosystem where Blacks and poor whites provided their bodies, their families, and muscle from sunup to sundown. After slavery, which banned education, labor was the only skill they had, the only life they knew, and it was a matter of survival. In the absence of real wages, sharecroppers survived on credit. Every spring, they went into debt, buying seed, clothes, food, and tools from the local merchant—usually at inflated prices, often owned or influenced by the same planter who owned the land.

This system was called the crop lien. It meant that until the crop was harvested and sold, all the proceeds from the field were pledged to repay these debts. If a family's cotton yield fetched $600 at the gin, and they owed the store $620, they started the next season $20 in debt. The cycle was repeated again and again. The accounts were always a mystery; the books were always conveniently off limits. Remember, the financial aspect was strictly the purview of the landowners. So even if the sharecroppers could read, they weren't allowed to review business records confirming their share of the income.

Families were trapped in cycles of subsistence farming and high-interest debt, ensuring the landowner profited, while the sharecropper hovered at or below the poverty line. Year after year, the crop lien system effectively eliminated mobility and created a caste system in America.

Backbreaking work was constant—bending, crouching, placing bolls in woven baskets or gunny sacks. Imagine a day spent bent over, dragging the increasingly heavy sack behind you as you pick up and down the rows. Sharecroppers "worked from can till can't" or from sunup to sundown. Children too young to tote a full-size sack picked in feed sacks, flour sacks, or pillowcases.

This was the life: Planting in early spring. Chopping weeds in summer. Picking cotton through the late, blistering Texas autumn. Fingers raw from boll spines. Children working alongside their parents because otherwise the crop wouldn't get picked. Your tenancy in the shack where you lived depended on the good graces of the landowner.

Sharecroppers lived in shotgun shacks with no insulation and leaky tin roofs. Malaria, dysentery, and pneumonia were common. Shoes were rare. Schooling was sporadic or nonexistent, especially during harvest season. Muscle mattered, not math.

A family might pick 200 to 300 pounds of cotton a day. A good hand might pick 400. For this, the market paid fifty cents to one dollar per 100 pounds, depending, of course, on market value and demand that season. Not per hour—for a day's work. With luck and perfect weather, a family might bring in $80 to $100 for the entire harvest. The money had to cover their debts and provide food through the winter.

Jim Crow laws dovetailed with sharecropping—reinforcing power hierarchies, providing economic leverage over labor, and keeping families in a state of semi-serfdom. Voting was suppressed. Power structures were closed. Violence, especially lynching, loomed as a constant threat to anyone who challenged the system.

Cotton is a part of my history. Cotton is part of my present. Part of my legacy is paving the way for future generations to understand the history of England, Ireland, Nigeria, and the Native Americans—our genealogy is mixed and beautiful.

I write this book because a life history is remembered if told—and dreams for future generations can begin if they know that someone else has made some steps in that direction. I hope my future grandchildren understand that they are part of a legacy that believes in big dreams, a work ethic, and strong values. Make sure you comb the cotton to be your best resilient self!

About the Author

Robin Wilson is an award-winning author, entrepreneur, and recognized pioneer in the allergen-aware wellness movement, known for translating science, design, and lifestyle into healthier homes and products. With a twenty-five-year entrepreneurial journey, she has built a global wellness brand that serves health-conscious, allergen-aware consumers through thoughtfully designed products and strategic partnerships with major retailers worldwide.

Wilson is the author of three books that reflect her leadership in wellness and design. Her debut, *Kennedy Green House* (2010), earned national recognition for its forward-thinking approach to healthy living. She followed with *Clean Design: Wellness for Your Lifestyle* (2015), a primer that helped define a new category of wellness-focused design, and hit #1 on the Amazon bestseller list.

Her third book, *Combing Cotton*, marks her twenty-fifth anniversary as an entrepreneur, shares her ancestry and inspiration, and focuses on resilience and wisdom to reach your best self.

Beyond publishing, Wilson is widely respected for her business acumen and cultural influence. In 2024, she received a Distinguished Alumni Award from New York University and delivered the convocation address at Radio City Music Hall. In 2020, she was named to *Inc.* magazine's Top 100 Female Founders and has received additional industry accolades for innovation and entrepreneurship. And in 2013, she was inducted in the Hall of Honor for Stephen F. Austin High School.

Wilson's work and insights have been featured on national television and in major media outlets, further amplifying her mission to improve everyday wellness. As a leading lifestyle brand, Clean Design Home® was founded by Robin Wilson and continues to shape the global conversation around allergen-aware living, empowering consumers to make healthier, more informed choices. Her lifestyle brand and work bridges wellness, design, and commerce with integrity, accessibility, and long-term global impact.

She is a native Texan and now lives in the metro-NYC area with her teen daughter. She is a graduate of New York University (MS) and the University of Texas at Austin (BA).